Binge Eating Disorder

Binge Eating Disorder, written by a clinician and an advocate who have personally struggled with Binge Eating Disorder (BED), illuminates the experience of BED from the patient perspective while also exploring the disorder's etiological roots and addressing the components of treatment that are necessary for long-term recovery. Accessible for both treatment providers and patients alike, this unique volume aims to explore BED treatment and recovery from both sides of the process while also providing a resource for structuring treatment and building effective interventions. This practical roadmap to understanding, resilience, and lasting change will be useful for anyone working clinically with or close to individuals suffering from BED, as well as those on the recovery journey.

Amy Pershing, LMSW, ACSW, is the founder of Bodywise™ binge eating disorder treatment program and clinical director of the Center for Eating Disorders in Ann Arbor, Michigan.

Chevese Turner is the founder of the Binge Eating Disorder Association (BEDA) and a passionate advocate and speaker working to eliminate eating disorders and weight stigma.

First published 2019
by Routledge
52 Vanderbilt Avenue, New York, NY 10017

and by Routledge
2 Park Square, Milton Park, Abingdon, Oxon, OX14 4RN

Routledge is an imprint of the Taylor & Francis Group, an informa business

© 2019 Taylor & Francis

Library of Congress Cataloging-in-Publication Data
Names: Pershing, Amy, author. | Turner, Chevese, author.
Title: Binge eating disorder : the journey to recovery and beyond / Amy Pershing with Chevese Turner.
Description: New York, NY : Routledge, 2018. | Includes bibliographical references and index.
Identifiers: LCCN 2018016004 (print) | LCCN 2018017283 (ebook) | ISBN 9781315301396 (eBook) | ISBN 9781138236929 (hbk) | ISBN 9781138236936 (pbk) | ISBN 9781315301396 (ebk)
Subjects: LCSH: Compulsive eating. | Compulsive eating—Treatment.
Classification: LCC RC552.C65 (ebook) | LCC RC552.C65 P47 2018 (print) | DDC 616.85/26—dc23
LC record available at https://lccn.loc.gov/2018016004

ISBN: 978-1-138-23692-9 (hbk)
ISBN: 978-1-138-23693-6 (pbk)
ISBN: 978-1-315-30139-6 (ebk)

Typeset in Warnock Pro
by Apex CoVantage, LLC

Binge Eating Disorder

The Journey to Recovery and Beyond

Amy Pershing with Chevese Turner

Routledge
Taylor & Francis Group

NEW YORK AND LONDON

To my husband Jeffrey Hoover for his unwavering love, to Judith Banker for being family of choice, and to my courageous clients who have allowed me to walk alongside them for a while on their journey home.

—Amy Pershing

To my husband Ryan Turner, for his love and support, and to my boys Aidan and Liam for teaching me about a love that has no boundaries.

—Chevese Turner

Ultimately, there is always the need to risk being new. Yet even succeeding, to be authentic—living as close to our experience as possible—is arduous. For being human, we remember and forget. We stray and return, fall down and get up, and cling and let go, again and again. But it is this straying and returning that makes life interesting, this clinging and letting go—damned as it is—that exercises the heart.

—Mark Nepo

Contents

About the Authors

Amy Pershing LMSW, ACSW is the Founding Director of Bodywise™, a comprehensive treatment program for binge eating disorder (BED), and Clinical Director of the Center for Eating Disorders in Ann Arbor, Michigan. She is the Founder of Hungerwise™, a 10-week program for ending chronic dieting and weight cycling.

Pershing lectures internationally and writes extensively on the treatment of BED and her own recovery journey for both professional and lay communities. She has been featured on numerous radio and television programs speaking about BED treatment and recovery, relapse prevention, weight stigma, and finding peace with food and movement. She has served on a variety of professional boards and is the Past Chair of the Binge Eating Disorder Association (BEDA). She is also the recipient of BEDA's Pioneer in Clinical Advocacy Award. In the field for nearly 30 years, Amy maintains her clinical practice in Ann Arbor.

Information about her programs and work can be found at thebodywiseprogram.com, hungerwise.com, and center4ed.org.

Chevese Turner is the Founder, President, and CEO of the Binge Eating Disorder Association (BEDA), a national organization promoting the pursuit of healing and well-being for those affected by binge eating disorder (BED).

Turner has a background in non-profit management, health care policy, and patient advocacy. She speaks regularly about her journey with BED, weight stigma, and the lack of recognition and access to care for those with eating disorders, and is regularly featured on podcasts, radio, and television. She currently sits on the board of the Academy of Eating Disorders (AED), is a past board member for the National Association of Anorexia Nervosa and Associated Disorders (ANAD), and has frequently served as team leader on National Lobby Days hosted by the Eating Disorders Coalition. Turner is the recipient of the AED's Meehan-Hartley Award for Public Service and Advocacy.

Information about Turner and BEDA can be found at BEDAonline.com and CheveseTurner.com.

Acknowledgments

Thanks to the clients and clinical professionals who have shared their journeys with us for this book, and to those who recognized and wrapped their arms around the BED community long before it was an official diagnosis. To all who struggle with an eating disorder but have not yet named their struggle as such, and to the many who lack access to informed treatment, your experiences are helping challenge us all in the treatment community to finally hear and serve everyone in need.

Thanks to Deb Burgard, Judith Matz, Theresa Chesnut, Carmen Cool, and Hilary Kinavey for their clinical contributions and advocacy efforts in this field. Thanks also to Jill Swenson, our developmental editor, and to Amanda Devine, our editor at Routledge, who believed in this book and helped guide it to publication.

Note to the Reader

The authors are grateful for the wisdom of many voices coming together to help create this book. People in all stages of recovery, clinical professionals who treat BED and co-occurring disorders, recovery advocates, scholars, and researchers have contributed to the following pages. It is our hope that members of each of these audiences will be able to take something new away in their reading as well. Each chapter opens with experiences from Chevese Turner about her personal recovery journey. The remaining portion of each chapter offers a clarifying lens into understanding why BED exists, and clinical strategies developed by Amy Pershing in her three decades as a psychotherapist. Throughout the chapters, the reader will also find quotes from colleagues and from Amy's clients. The names of many of these contributors have been withheld to protect confidentiality. Their powerful and courageous voices contribute to the points in the text.

The book in its entirety, read in the order presented, is written to be of benefit to those in recovery and those taking first steps in the process. For clinicians treating BED, we hope the book will be both a useful tool in treatment planning as well as a source of education regarding many of the myths about BED and definitions of recovery. For scholars and researchers, we hope this book will generate ideas for further directions of study, particularly with regard to BED and the neurological impact of trauma (Chapter 2). Nutrition professionals and coaches may benefit particularly from Chapters 1, 4, and 5. Clinicians new to BED treatment and those who support BED recovery will benefit in particular from the information in Chapter 1.

The authors have made every effort throughout this book to be as welcoming to all readers as possible. For many, lack of access to health care, lack of time available to devote to recovery efforts, and limited availability of BED-informed treatment providers negatively affect access to resources essential for healing. Poverty, racism, misogyny, homophobia, gender binarism, ableism, and lack of multicultural awareness profoundly impact recovery for many with BED. The authors address these barriers whenever possible, and seek to offer some hope and guidance for incorporating advocacy efforts into the process of healing. The authors would also like to acknowledge both our journeys of recovery, and careers in this field, have been significantly aided by the privilege we enjoy.

1

Cookies Under the Floorboards and Doritos Under the Bed

I woke to the hum and hiss of the window air conditioner in my little room with pink walls. As my feet hit the wooden floors, the ruffles on my princess nightgown that bunched up around my waist during the night slid down my legs, I began to smell the heat from a pan of boiling water on the electric stove and knew this meant my least favorite breakfast.

Mom stood at the kitchen sink with her back to me. Dressed in her bell-bottom blue jeans and a flowery peasant shirt, she was medium height. Her dark brown hair curled around her face and she wore glasses with large frames.

"Good morning Chev. Get ready for breakfast. We are having Cream of Wheat."

I made a face. Ew.

"It's good for you. You aren't going to eat a bunch of sugary junk for breakfast that will make you fat," Mom said.

I took my seat at the table and sat quietly.

My younger brother began to protest and pushed his bowl away. "I want sumpin' else. I want sumpin' else!"

In exasperation, Mom made him eggs while I nibbled at my Cream of Wheat.

I picked up my bowl and emptied the barely eaten breakfast in to the trash. I ran to my room, changed into shorts and a shirt that showed part of my stomach. I was ready to run out the door when my mother stopped me in my tracks.

"I'm not sure you should wear that shirt. Your stomach is too big for it now."

I turned around and walked slowly back up the stairs. Suddenly my body felt weak and by the time I made it to my closet to find something else to wear, I no longer felt the urge to run outside and play with friends. The lull of the air conditioner appealed more to me than playing in the heat outside. I flopped down on to the mattress with my shoe-clad feet hanging over the side. I began to feel sleepy and my stomach gurgled.

"Chevese, hurry up and get outside," Mom yelled from the kitchen.

I knew the drill—get outside and run around as much as possible until lunchtime. I pulled myself up from the bed and thought about how the inside of my upper legs would rub together when I ran and how much I wanted to have smaller legs like Katie who lived down the street. I wondered if Katie worried about being like her mom who was so fat she had to wear shapeless, ugly dresses to cover her large body. I wondered what it would be like to be that fat. I knew my mom worried I would be like Katie's mom.

My friends had waited for me in the backyard. The previous afternoon we had set up a makeshift theatre for a puppet show and this was the day we would invite our parents to attend. Katie and the new girl, Anna, who recently moved in to the house behind ours, were impatient to begin practicing our skit.

"Come on heavy Chevy, you can run," Katie yelled at me. I recognized the nickname her older brother had given me earlier that summer.

We practiced our puppet show the remainder of the morning until it was time for lunch. My brother and I ran to the door leading in to the kitchen, threw it open, and proclaimed we were starving.

"You are always hungry," Mom laughed and rolled her eyes.

My stomach rumbled in a way that was painful and I could think of nothing but food. I sat down at the table and waited patiently as my mother prepared sandwiches. As she made her way toward the table, I could see something red sticking out between the two slices of whole wheat bread and knew what this meant: tomato sandwiches! My heart sank. I was so hungry and hated tomatoes. "Mom, can I have peanut butter and jelly instead of a tomato sandwich?" I asked.

"Absolutely not. This is what we are having. Tomatoes are good for you. Jelly is full of sugar," she replied.

I gagged on the first bite and nibbled the bread around the tomato.

"If you do not eat the tomato, then you won't get any of the pudding I made for dessert tonight," Mom said.

I left the tomato minus the bread crust on the plate.

"You must begin to eat healthy foods or you will be fat. I love you, but I don't want that for you," she said.

I wanted to cry. I did not like Cream of Wheat or tomatoes. I was hungry and yet my upper legs rubbed together. *I'm five and destined to be fat.*

I found myself alone in the kitchen while Mom was in the basement doing laundry. My stomach gurgled and my brain felt foggy. What was in the cabinets of our kitchen that could make this awful feeling go away? I found a box of cones used for ice cream treats. I grabbed them and ran quickly to my room, my heart beating as it never had before. I hid the cones under my bed and walked quickly out the door to join my friends.

The remainder of the afternoon crept by as my mind continually returned to the contraband under my bed. The anticipation of filling my stomach in the cool air of my bedroom distracted me from the things I loved to do with my friends: riding bike, tag, and preparing for the puppet show for our siblings and parents.

Closing my bedroom door enough to provide cover in case someone came down the hall, I pulled the box from beneath the bed and opened it far enough to slide out a single cone. The cake cone was dry and tasteless, but I frantically ate as many cones as possible until the box was almost empty. My stomach was full. I felt content and warm all over. I laid back on my bed as the air conditioner hummed. *What would Mom say when she noticed the ice cream cones missing?* I would need to keep my secret well-hidden and lie if necessary.

"Chevese! It's time for dinner," my mother yelled from the kitchen. I rolled to my side as I began to sit up. I felt groggy and my head hurt. My stomach felt bloated and my legs and arms were heavy. I stood up and began to walk out of the bedroom, shuffling down the hall slowly. I already regretted eating the ice cream cones.

I greeted my family and sat down at my usual place at the table. Dad asked, "Do you feel well? You look like you are sick."

"My stomach hurts," I replied. "I'm not hungry."

"OK, then why don't you go get ready for bed," Mom suggested.

I stood up and made my way to my bedroom. I put on my princess nightgown, got into bed, and pulled the covers high around my neck. My stomach churned and I thought about the ice cream cone box that remained under my bed. Tomorrow I would find a way to put the box into the trash or in a place Mom would never think to look.

This can never happen again. Never.

▶ A SAVING GRACE

Three to five million people struggle with binge eating disorder. BED is three times more common than anorexia and bulimia combined, and more common than breast cancer, HIV, and schizophrenia. It is not about diet failure, personal weakness, or lack of willpower. BED is not only for young, privileged white women, as eating disorders are often misunderstood to be. Those of us who know binge eating disorder know a relationship with food that is fraught with confusion, contradiction, and shame. Food is an enemy in certain ways—something that triggers guilt-ridden thoughts, worry about sticking to a food plan, "cheating" on a diet, and gaining (or regaining) weight. But food is also a safe haven, a brief disconnection and respite from the toughest parts of life, both past and present.

As a psychotherapist who specializes in BED treatment, I have seen some incredible people come through my office doors in the last 30 years in a desperate search for help to stop binge eating. My clients, like most with BED, are resilient, capable, and strong—although they do not typically see themselves this way. They come from all walks of life, all ages, colors, beliefs, physical abilities, genders, socioeconomic groups, and sexual orientations. They are every shape and size. Many have survived extraordinary hardships. They usually feel a terrible shame about their eating disorder, but know it has somehow provided a safe hiding place that belongs to them, and them alone:

> When I decide to binge, I'm free. There is nothing like it. I can feel my body relax and then kind of disappear. Then I see the evening ahead of me. Just me, the TV, and the food, then sleep. A kind of sleep you can't get without bingeing. There won't be room for anything, or anyone, else. I won't think about all the things I'm going to screw up tomorrow, or who doesn't like me, or who is going to leave me.

> "I have always hidden food." "Knowing it's there calms me."

> "A freight train couldn't have stopped me from eating."

> "This is my way out of here."

> "I'd lose my mind if I had to stop and think. Worse yet, stop and feel."

Like Chevese and my clients, I have also walked my own path with binge eating, struggling for almost two decades before coming out the other side. Healing BED is not an easy journey; my recovery, in all its imperfection, has required courage, commitment, and risk. I have learned some surprising things along the way. I have found what matters most to long-term change is the ability to turn gently inward when I struggle, tell the truth of my inner and outer experience, learn to allow myself to be seen and cared for in healthy connection with others, treat my body as my home, and to fight back against the cultural forces that would otherwise undermine my efforts at recovery. It is a complicated path, and an ongoing one, but it is also life giving, and probably the most profound thing I will ever do.

As with most eating disorders, there is often significant body shame for those of us with BED, regardless of actual body size; trying to look thinner or hide our bodies are ubiquitous parts of everyday life. As for most women in our culture, with or without BED, disliking our body feels *normal*. Many with BED have lived through weight-related bullying, and judgments from family, partners, doctors and other health professionals, and society at large. We have often had at best only brief and fleeting moments of being at peace with our bodies, typically predicated on weight loss or shape change. Most of us have yo-yo dieted, sometimes for years, ashamed of our ongoing and very public "failures."

For people struggling with binge eating, there is desperate hope the behavior will somehow stop, and the nightmare emotional rollercoaster will end. There is much promise, propagated by well-oiled marketing efforts, that the newest weight loss plan will be successful. Time and again, however, this desire for change will be thwarted by the overwhelming drive to eat. Without an understanding of what is really going on psychologically and physiologically, the urge to binge will remain far more powerful than the hope to stop. In fact, as we will discover, binge eating is an extraordinarily *adaptive* behavior that becomes entrenched with time and repetition. By the time people seek treatment, binge eating rarely feels like much of a "choice" anymore. One of my clients said it this way: "My decision to binge is not a conscious choice in the moment. For me, binge eating feels like I'm outrunning the floodwaters of my life. Eating produces a sensation of shelter."

I first sought my own treatment for binge eating—very reluctantly and with much embarrassment—more than 35 years ago. Back in the early eighties, there was no label for my behavior patterns with food. One therapist even referred to me as a "failed bulimic" because I didn't purge. I had no idea recovery would mean not only a change in my eating, but, more critically, developing an understanding of all that was driving my binges in the first place. Despite no official diagnosis, I knew this *was* a distinct eating disorder.

Like bulimia, I ate uncontrollably, despite using every ounce of willpower I possessed to make it stop. Regardless of my many efforts at white knuckling, binge episodes were frequent and frantic, but also trance-like and disconnected from the world around me. I often planned a binge, sometimes looking forward to it all day until I could eat. It felt like a huge relief, finally letting go of something heavy, a weight lifted. Unlike bulimia however, my binge eating was not followed by any kind of purging behavior. It was followed instead by intense self-recrimination and judgment for succumbing yet again.

In the rest of my life, when I set my mind on something, I achieved it. Most projects and goals happened as planned. I was exceptionally lucky in many ways. I was safe. I had food and shelter. I was not being threatened or in immediate danger. I am white, heterosexual, and able-bodied. Even with such a level of privilege, nothing seemed to touch that drive to binge. I looked to the world like someone high-functioning and capable. Yet when that craving to eat kicked in, there seemed to be no way anything could stop it. Even the *thought* of stopping during a binge filled me with anxiety, dread, and sadness. I could not deal with how badly I would feel if I stopped to notice. So, once it started, I had to see it through to the end.

I had a long history of dieting and losing weight, followed by stretches of evening after evening eating thousands of calories while watching TV. My mind would go numb to the promise I made the night before to *never* do this again. When I finally sought help, I felt very clear that I was there to get on track, to get my eating under control, and to get back to the business of looking and performing at my best (meaning losing weight and being "thin"). I needed strategies to stop my craziness and shape up, literally. I had no idea then that it was this very way of seeing my relationship with food (and myself) that was actually making a binge *much more likely*. It took many years of my own healing, and clinical training as a therapist, to truly learn what works for recovery. It was both far simpler, and far more difficult, than I could have imagined. And very much worth the effort.

When I began my clinical career, BED didn't even have a name, much less an official diagnosis. If the binge behavior was even identified by any health care professional, it was "treated" with a "sensible" diet, a lecture about staying the course, and tips for working on developing more willpower. Best case, it was considered an issue of working on bad body thoughts and negative self-talk, something easily addressed by a few structured sessions of cognitive-behavioral psychotherapy. Certainly this is what insurance companies, when they covered eating disorders at all, might have had us believe. Bottom line: the disorder was somehow the fault of the client, and could be addressed by some simple strategic interventions. Ending binge behavior defined recovery. It was not understood that this is just one step on the journey, necessary but not sufficient for long-term change. There was only cursory exploration of what the behavior might be about psychologically or how it might serve a critical function. Additionally, there was little understanding about the impact of dieting on BED, or how our cultural ideas about weight and shape actually inflict trauma and *lead* to binge behaviors. Given huge rates of relapse, achieving and maintaining long-term recovery seemed elusive to clinicians. Therapists used to speak of the "resistance of BED clients to change." Thankfully, through much hard work and dedication by committed clinical professionals and advocates, times have changed.

▶ WHAT'S IN A NAME?

Binge eating behaviors have had a number of names over time: emotional eating, compulsive overeating, and more recently, binge eating disorder (BED). While the terms have historically often been used interchangeably in the popular press, I would suggest a differentiation is valuable in understanding the comparative severity of BED, and the necessity for well-informed, effective treatment. As I use the terms in my clinical work (and in this book), emotional eating and compulsive eating are periodic, episodic uses of food in *times of stress* to manage significant emotions. They are very common behaviors when food is plentiful. They are relatively short-lived, and the episodes are somewhat conscious decisions. Picture eating a carton of ice cream after a breakup, or eating a box of cookies in one sitting when worried about a work situation or conflict with a friend. Such life events may trigger the desire to soothe or distract with food. But, once the stressor is passed, eating goes back to normal levels. There is little guilt about the episode, mood remains basically positive, and the person is minimally affected psychologically by this bump in the coping road. For most people, such episodes are not anxiety producing or frequent enough to seek intervention. If they do look for help, learning new skills for self-talk and some strategies for a more peaceful relationship with food and weight are typically enough to make effective change.

Binge eating disorder is fundamentally different. It is far more entrenched in a person's life than emotional or compulsive eating. BED is typically of significantly longer duration, begins earlier in life, and is more complex to change. Eating episodes are more severe and more frequent. There is a higher incidence of overwhelming life experiences that impact the development of the behaviors. There is a much greater sense of a lack of control over the binge; episodes feel more impulsive. Those with BED tend to be more "checked out" during a binge (clinically referred to as "dissociation"). They may face significant depression and anxiety, histories of trauma or loss, and profound struggles with body image (regardless of size). The binge cycles in BED are more difficult to treat with simple techniques for challenging negative thinking, or changes made only in relationship to food. Something more in-depth and comprehensive is needed for change to happen, and to stick.

When BED is present, a binge offers effective disconnection from pain, shame, or fear:

> Food thoughts and planning a binge gave me a safe harbor when I was afraid or lonely. It got me through my past, my divorce, and a whole lot of pain I had no idea how to address.

> I get up from wherever I am when feelings begin to overwhelm me. I binge eat until I feel a bit more calm, or until guilt requires me to put it away. I go back to where I was sitting or working, and then, sometimes even moments later, I get up, walk into the kitchen, open the cabinets, remove the rubber band from the package and begin again. Spooning food into emotional upheaval somehow brings momentary relief.

This relationship with food repeatedly brings respite from a psychological place that seems, in that moment, impossible to withstand:

> Usually the urge happens when I'm thinking about something upsetting or uncomfortable. My thoughts drift to what bad foods I have to eat. It's a seemingly innocent line of thought. Something like, oh, what could make me feel better right now? And then the decision comes quickly and overwhelmingly. Once I've committed to bingeing I need to do it as soon as possible. The blinders come on and as soon as I'm in the house I'm reaching for whatever I can.

For most with BED, a binge is frenetic, impulse-driven, and feels impossible to waylay:

> It's eating fast. Shoveling food in. It tastes so good. I want more. It's taking another bite—and another, and another—while still chewing the first bite. It's barely chewing. It's swallowing hard, fast. I tell myself I'll only eat until—fill in the blank—until this row, this section, this portion, is gone. I'll only even out this layer of ice cream, I'll get it even with the writing on the side of the carton. But more is never enough. And

I deserve it. It's been a long day. It's late. I'm tired. I'll exercise more. Soon. Tomorrow. Next week. I'll make up for it.

The decision is sudden. It's like blinders are put on and all I can think about is the plan to binge. My mind goes blank, and it's as though I unplug from my body and the world around me. Usually there is some sort of emotional discomfort before I first experience the drive to binge, and then the decision comes as a relief to soothe whatever uneasiness I feel.

I know I am tired of performing, of getting everything right everywhere. Binge eating is a way to do *nothing right*. In a weird way it makes me feel powerful for a moment. Then it comes crashing down, and I feel totally out of control.

When I binge eat, the decision feels like what I imagine an alcoholic or heroin addict feels—I need a fix. I first experience the urge to binge eat physically. I start to feel anxious in my stomach. I feel a gnawing deep in my belly right above my belly button, but it's not hunger. It's feelings of anxiety and self-doubt and worry. I think of it as a mini-tornado in my stomach twisting and turning furiously and growing bigger and gaining strength until I make it go away with food. I need food to make uncomfortable and painful feelings go away. I want to numb out and distract myself from whatever emotional discomfort I am experiencing. The feelings are intolerable and I have to make them stop.

Importantly for many with BED, binge eating can also serve as a powerful act of rebellion. Particularly when needs went unmet or feelings were historically unwelcome, the act of breaking rules and not meeting others' needs and expectations is actually a symbolically protective act. Rebellion from the culture of body shame in the form of binge eating can be a powerful, if secret (and thereby seemingly safer), act of defiance. It is a way of hanging on to the truth that something is *wrong*, that there is a real problem in the person's world, even if no one else knows or sees:

For me, binge eating was the one thing that was completely mine. When I first entered treatment, I felt two very different things. Part of me was ready to change. The other part was very clearly saying no way am I doing what I'm *supposed* to do.

I do know there are times I eat when I'm angry. Or when I feel self-loathing. Knowing I'm not healthy, that I'm struggling with pre-diabetes, with autoimmune issues, with food allergies, with high cholesterol. And I binge anyway. In spite of it. To spite it. To spite myself. To spite life. To spite God. To make it worse. Because I feel so, so, so bad. And sometimes feeling worse kind of helps me express the anger.

Binge eating can be a way to both *hold on to* and *quiet* one's true voice at the same time. Bingeing can be a way to resist attempts to be controlled or silenced, but to do it without anyone's knowledge. In fact, for some, binge eating is in itself a way to break rules and take power back from diets, and from other's expectations for weight loss:

> Binge eating was my way of saying no to my mother pushing me to lose weight. I didn't see it then, but now I know my weight was the best way for me to hold onto my own body.

> All day long I do what I'm supposed to do. But when I binge, I can let go of all the restrictions.

> After being bullied at school, I basically decided to fight all the time. For me, binge eating kept away feeling sad and vulnerable. I couldn't risk hearing my heart.

Recovery is not about *stopping* rebellion energy. Quite to the contrary, it is about developing the ability to hear and express it more powerfully and effectively. The energy behind rebellion can allow us to care for ourselves, to live in an authentic body, to set and keep limits and boundaries, and to make space for needs and feelings. Defiance is sometimes the best proof to ourselves that we exist, and that we have power at all. Recovery is about redirecting this determination to survive and flourish; it is not about being "good" and sticking to your diet. It is about being true to yourself and your own path. Any work to change must take the adaptive functions of BED into account, and address the underlying needs in other ways. To expect lasting change without this work is to truly misunderstand the nature of BED.

▶ THE SIZE OF THE PROBLEM

There are still so many misconceptions about BED. Do millions of people really have this disorder? Why isn't it simply a matter of behavioral changes? Why don't diets work as a solution for BED? And what does recovery really mean? Can it last?

Binge eating disorder is the most common eating disorder in the United States by fivefold. While the majority of people with eating disorders are female, binge eating disorder is the most common eating disorder among men. Some estimates suggest up to 40 percent of people with clinically diagnosable BED are male. Additionally, 30 to 40 percent of people seeking all types of weight loss treatments can be clinically diagnosed with the disorder, and up to 70 percent seeking bariatric surgeries meet diagnostic criteria. Three out of ten individuals looking for other weight loss treatments show signs of BED. Most (but not all) with BED have struggled with weight or body image issues or both. Many with BED are also burdened with other mental health concerns. Of those with BED, 60 percent struggle with *at least one* other diagnosable mental health issue, including PTSD, depression, and anxiety disorders.

Sadly, the misconception that lack of adequate willpower is a causal factor in BED actually fuels the disorder, reinforcing the shame and stopping people from getting the help they truly need to make lasting change. It has been many years of hard work by advocates, clinicians, and researchers for BED to be recognized as a *real* disorder, with severity and life impact on par with anorexia and bulimia. Such recognition is critical for insurance coverage and for research dollars to be allocated for treatment and prevention efforts. Recognition is also, perhaps most significantly to those with the disorder, a validation for the profound, enduring impact of BED on their lives. Prior to this development, BED was typically categorized as a "sub-clinical" disorder or an "unspecified" eating disorder. Or it was diagnosed as a symptom of something else, such as anxiety or depression. The recognition in the eating disorder community of BED as its own disorder gives voice to literally millions of people's experiences. It has been a critical development in helping those with BED understand the need for treatment and come to know that recovery is indeed possible.

The official clinical definition of BED can now be found in the *Diagnostic and Statistical Manual of Mental Disorders* (DSM-V). According to the DSM-V, BED is characterized by a number of behavioral and emotional symptoms:

▶ Recurrent episodes of binge eating occurring at least once a week for 3 months

▶ Eating a larger amount of food than would be considered "normal" during a short time frame

▶ Feeling out of control/unable to stop the binge episode

Binge eating episodes are also associated with three or more of the following:

▶ Eating until feeling uncomfortably full

▶ Eating large amounts of food when not physically hungry

▶ Eating much more rapidly than normal

▶ Eating alone out of embarrassment over quantity eaten

▶ Feeling disgusted, depressed, ashamed, or guilty after overeating

A critical hallmark of BED is feeling a *lack of control* over the episode. This may be the single most important difference diagnostically between BED and the overeating everyone does on occasion. Binge eating is something a person feels *compelled* to do, despite the shame that follows. The drive to do it overpowers the conviction not to time and again:

> I already feel bad about a binge before I even begin because I know I won't be able to stop it. It feels like a foregone conclusion before I take the first bite.

> I feel the drive in my body. My gut clenches, my muscles tighten. I know I'm about to binge, and I'm not going to let any thoughts about tomorrow stop me. It's like I'm another person.

This supposed lack of control in BED is, for many, driven by something basic and powerful. It, surprisingly, is a drive that makes sense, given the circumstances in which it develops. Humans are genetically and biochemically wired to find ways to cope with the environment, and binge eating is a very effective tool in certain circumstances and where other options are less viable or dependable. BED is not, therefore, about willpower or character, nor is it a result of pathology. It is often an inherent drive to survive and feel safe by disconnecting from fear and shame. The good news for recovery is that our neurological wiring as humans, and our ways of coping, truly can change. But it requires the right approach, one informed with a clear understanding of how humans naturally deal with adversity and fear.

▶ WHAT CAUSES BED?

There are many factors that combine to create the right circumstances for BED to occur, and we will explore them more fully throughout this book. Genetics may play a part, impacting a person's particular responses to stressors, how emotions are experienced, or how one copes with trauma and loss. There seem to be genetic predispositions to black-and-white thinking, perfectionism, and impulsivity, all common factors in BED. There may also be a genetic predisposition to dissociation, a hallmark of BED for many.

Problems with family or other significant relationships, significant losses, histories of emotional abuse, physical neglect, and sexual abuse are more correlated with BED than other eating disorders, and considerably higher than in the general population. Depression, anxiety, and other mood disorders, and struggles with addiction, are also correlated with BED. These co-occurring disorders may well arise as a combination of both genes and environment, and make BED that much more likely.

In addition, a third critical factor in the development of BED is a history of dieting, restrictive or irregular eating patterns, and a history of significant weight changes. People who have experienced weight-related discrimination and bullying are also more likely to have BED. These issues are especially prevalent for people in higher weight bodies with BED. The glorification and celebration of being thin in mainstream culture and popular media exacerbates this invisible problem shared by people of all sizes, races, classes, gender, religions, and identities. One response to environmental stressors of body shame, dieting, and weight-related bullying is soothing the pain and shame with binge eating.

▶ WHEN DOES BED BEGIN?

BED often begins in the late teens or early 20s, although it has been reported in both young children and older adults. In one study, 45 percent of the subjects reported dieting preceded their first binge episode and 55 percent reported binge eating preceded their first diet. The group reporting having binged first had a younger age of onset and a younger age at which they met diagnostic criteria. This group of people with BED who reported an early onset and were diagnosed at a younger age also were more like to have had a history of psychiatric problems. It is likely that an early age, pre-dieting onset is correlated with environmental and genetic causal factors. While dieting is definitely associated with the disorder, for those with pre-diet onset, dieting is more likely to be a reaction to binge behavior, rather than a cause.

▶ WHO STRUGGLES WITH BED?

BED is not confined to the eating disorder stereotype of young, white women. Approximately 40 percent of those with binge eating disorder are male. Additionally, over the past few years, there has been evidence of significant disordered eating across racial and ethnic minorities. Analysis of the Minnesota Adolescent Health Study found dieting, a common precursor to BED, was associated with weight dissatisfaction, seeing oneself as "overweight," and low body pride in *all* ethnic groups (French et al., 1997). Exact statistics on the prevalence of eating disorders among women of color are still largely unavailable. Additionally, more research is needed to determine if the experience of the disorder is the same for people from different food cultures and differing genetic makeup.

Environmental race-based stress for people of color can trigger the onset of disordered eating patterns as well. Among women of color, the process of acculturation can be one such source of stress. "By definition, acculturation is the process by which one group asserts its influence over another. The result is likely to be difficult, reactive, and conflictual, affecting one's physical and psychological functioning," according to Davis and Katzman (1999). The dominant images of femininity in mainstream culture are still thin, white, and young. Body ideals and social and cultural expectations vary, and more research will help us determine the nuances of the clinical picture.

Sexual orientation can be a contributing factor in developing BED as well. There remain significant dangers in coming out, including fear of rejection, discrimination, bullying and violence. Stigma and shame from non-binary gender expressions or transgender identity are common. Body image ideals within some LGBTQ communities may also contribute to body shame. Differences in rates of binge eating within the LGBTQ community have yet to be described in the research, but one thing is clear: many of these factors can be traumatic, and trauma, as we will see, sharply increases vulnerability to an eating disorder.

Poverty and food scarcity can also significantly impact the development of binge eating behavior. Research shows an increased prevalence of various eating disorder features, particularly binge eating, in people who are unemployed or underemployed. Poverty is especially hard on young children. The stress and hardship that goes along with growing up poor can cause a child to cope in unhealthy ways, and food may well be one of few available soothing mechanisms. If food itself is scarce or unpredictable, enforced cycles of restriction (as with intentional behavioral weight loss programs) can in and of themselves increase the likelihood of binge eating when food is available.

"Food deserts" are common in areas of socioeconomic depression. Food deserts are geographic areas in which access to affordable, healthy food options (especially fresh fruits and vegetables) is restricted or nonexistent due to the absence of grocery stores within a practical traveling distance. Sometimes these are also areas of "food swamps," so named because these communities are flooded with unhealthy, highly processed, low-nutrient food combined with disproportionate advertising for such foods compared to wealthier neighborhoods. The moralization of food and food choices combined with limited access to abundant, affordable food choices adds to shame and guilt. This internalized self-blame can further fuel binge eating. Worse yet, "fitness deserts"—areas without the infrastructure or safe places for affordable exercise—make it more difficult for low-income people to access safe, enjoyable movement options. Finally, because poverty and the medicalization of fat are also intimately linked, eating disorders among people living in poverty often fly well under the radar of identification. Lack of access to affordable screening and treatment is another significant blow to attempts at recovery.

People of all shapes and sizes struggle with BED. We cannot assume the presence of binge eating if someone is considered overweight, nor can we dismiss the possibility of binge eating behaviors if someone is in the "normal", or even underweight categories. Simply stated, we cannot tell by looking who does or does not struggle with BED.

Ultimately, BED can impact people in many walks of life. What clinicians see most across the demographic spectrum is the presence of high levels of anxiety and shame. Sometimes the sociocultural perceptions of these demographics, not the demographic itself, can be the *cause* of much of the anxiety and shame experienced. Recovery is in part healing the impact of stigma, and finding a community of support with whom we can safely question and challenge the dominant paradigms.

▶ IS BED AN ADDICTION?

There is a clinical paradigm that suggests binge eating is an addiction, and as such, should be treated using a 12-Step/abstinence model, much as one would with any other addictive substance or behavior. The theory suggests the brain experiences a dopamine surge during a binge much as with other drugs such as cocaine or heroin. Thus, abstinence, including the avoidance of many food ingredients (often sugar and gluten among them) is the only way for long-term change.

In my own recovery, I spent about 8 years in Overeaters Anonymous. Going to many meetings each week and talking with my sponsor, I worked a program that varied from a very tightly controlled eating plan (called "Gray Sheet") to one that was more flexible and adaptive (but still included calorie counting and measured portions). In either case, I was expected to call my sponsor each morning and commit my eating plan for the day. Given that I could not be trusted with food choices in the moment, I had to make these decisions ahead of time with a witness to hold me accountable. The program required I surrender to a higher power, confess to wrongdoings against those I had hurt during my "disease," and other various restitutions as prescribed by the 12 Steps. Despite this long-sought clear path to end my bingeing, however, I inevitably went back to it, with the shame and hopelessness even more convincing than before. With the latest binge, I not only dealt with whatever stressors may have been part of the initial need to go to food, but also with the knowledge I had broken my abstinence. I had to start over, day one, yet again shown to be powerless over this substance. Finally, I gave up. We treat few other medical conditions with such moralizing as we do addiction—admitting powerlessness is rarely seen as a necessary part of healing. This idea fits in perfectly, however, with the blame-the-victim approach and concurrent cultural assumption of lack of willpower as the culprit.

There are many other reasons that an addiction model does not effectively describe causes of BED or suggest effective treatments. One theory, the dopamine model, purports that, as with substances like cocaine, when dopamine is released as a result of use, one has feelings of pleasure or satisfaction. To satisfy that desire, the person will repeat behaviors that cause the release of dopamine. When food is the substance, an abstinence model intrinsically presents some challenges.

First, we are dopamine-seeking creatures inherently. This is not pathological, but hardwired. We experience dopamine surges in many ways, including listening to music, reading a good book, or playing with puppies. Food and sex also naturally trigger dopamine release. Thus, sugar is not intrinsically a substance, using addiction parlance, any more than a hug from a friend would be. Both are sources of dopamine release. For most people with BED, there are other issues (anxiety, depression, trauma histories, unmet needs of many kinds) that drive them to seek ways to feel better. This is not physiological *addiction*; it is a survival response to control anxiety and shame.

In a survey conducted by Gearhardt and colleagues (2009) at Yale, findings initially supported the theory of food addiction. Yet, as we look closely, the questionnaire seems to possibly measure something else entirely. Here is a sample of the items in the instrument.

▶   I find myself consuming certain foods even though I am no longer hungry.

▶   I worry about cutting down on certain foods.

▶   I have spent time dealing with negative feelings from overeating certain foods, instead of spending time in important activities such as time with family, friends, work, or recreation.

Each of these experiences can be attributed to the effects of chronic dieting. It is impossible to diagnose addiction when the substance of choice has been unnaturally restricted. A 2016 literature review in the *European Journal of Nutrition* looked at the evidence on highly processed foods with high sugar content and found that addiction-like behaviors such as binge eating occurred only when subjects had previously been restricted from sugar.

The review's authors state, "These behaviours likely arise from intermittent access to sweet tasting or highly palatable foods, not the neurochemical effects of sugar" (Westwater, 2016). Additionally, there are three studies to date in which binge eaters are asked to eat their forbidden foods as part of the treatment process. In each of them, binge eating decreased significantly. Surprising results if food were an addiction.

What I have observed in my clinical experience, over and over, is this: the effects of deprivation due to dieting are far and away the biggest contributor to increasing the reward value of food. Neither our bodies nor our minds make a distinction between a diet and a famine. In any food plan that requires either making certain foods forbidden or demands the experience of sustained hunger, we will be far more likely to think about those forbidden foods, seek them out, and overeat them given the opportunity. There is research that suggests when we are deprived and excessively hungry, the hormones that signal fullness decrease and the hormones that signal hunger, particularly leptin, increase. This is not addiction. It is our bodies' appropriate response to a perceived threat to survival. This is a completely different chemical and neurological process than the physiological dependence created by the use of narcotic drugs or alcohol.

Clinically and personally, I see that having permission and opportunity to eat all foods from a place of body awareness significantly lessens binge episodes. The vast majority of my clients with BED either do not know their body's true food needs, or ignore those needs in a constant effort to lose weight. The drive to be thin (and the accompanying shame if they are not) typically supersedes any attempt to listen to hunger, fullness, or satiety. When my clients eat foods without restriction (including those forbidden ingredients like sugar and gluten) and truly learn to listen to their body's desire from a place of acceptance, they eat in a nutrition-rich, and sustainable way *most of the time.* An addiction model prescribes the very thing that keeps people stuck: a fundamental belief that they cannot be trusted with food decisions and cannot endure moderation. I find the exact opposite to be true. Building body awareness, trust, and acceptance leads to long-term change, and the ability to eat without some externally devised set of rules. It is essentially eating as the body is designed, making choices based on need in the moment, desire, appetite, and overall body awareness. We are finally seeing a growing body of research that backs this up, and even more is on the horizon.

There are often rituals that accompany binge eating, such as going to the same place each time, eating at the same time of day, or watching TV or being on the computer while eating. These patterns are sometimes referred to as a "process addiction." They are typically deeply entrenched with binge eating behaviors, and on their own can trigger an episode. If a certain TV show comes on, or even simply upon entering the house after work, environmental triggers can elicit thoughts about bingeing. These patterns do need to be addressed in treatment, but they can be changed by helping clients gain greater awareness, intervening early in the pattern, and learning other ways to soothe. Such behaviors are not addictions: they are part of the distraction that quiets the voice of shame about eating that which is forbidden.

▶ CRAVING AND RITUAL

The craving to binge feels unstoppable and overwhelming. In describing their cravings to binge, my clients talk of obsessive thoughts about certain foods, body sensations of muscle tension, and feelings of both excitement and dread. For some of my clients, there are also feelings of rebellion or self-destruction that are expressed by giving in to a binge:

> It's like standing on the edge of a cliff. The last thing you should do is jump. You know that. You have jumped before and deeply regretted it. And yet you feel absolutely compelled to do just that.

Others describe a "click" into binge mode and the sense they are almost overtaken by the desire. Many people describe a sense of relief once they decide to eat:

> When I finally do decide to binge, it feels like the fight is over. That fight is exhausting, and for a moment, I'm actually relieved.

> To binge or not to binge: it is not really a *discussion*. It's a reaction. A driven-ness. A disconnect from conscious, thoughtful decision making.

Perhaps not surprisingly, binge eating is neurologically an effective temporary strategy for the reduction of anxiety. For us humans, the reduction of fear is a far greater drive than almost anything else. Said plainly, in the moment, binge eating works.

There are often strong patterns and a sense of ritual in binge eating behaviors. People may go to many of the same foods (or types of foods) for binges, and may favor different foods for different situations or moods. People with BED usually have specific places they binge that, as noted above, may in and of themselves trigger the desire to eat. In addition, most people do other activities at the same time, such as watch television, get on the computer, or read. Many people have favorite shows, websites, or books they have usually gone to many times before. It is rare for people to binge without a distraction, thus quieting the small voice that might hope to *stop* the behavior. It allows the experience of checking out of the world to be more complete:

> I come home and turn on my binge shows before I have a chance to decide not to do it. I put on my loosest clothes, turn off the phone, and eat. I want salty then sweet, in that order, over and over. It's the same pattern, every time.

> Any time I am around certain foods, chips especially, I will binge. They are a mainstay for me. If I'm buying them, I know I'm preparing to binge. I just push down that feeling of shame and eat, knowing (but not caring) that the same shame will slam me when I stop.

> Sometimes, as I move toward a binge stash, I might perceive a gentle, restraining hand on my arm, which I as much as slap away, feeling, although not articulating something adolescent like "Leave me alone! I'm doing this!"

As I often say to my clients, no one binges in front of a mirror. We cannot be truly connected to ourselves at a deep level and go through with a binge. It is essential to shut down the small voice that knows what the aftermath of the binge will be in order to continue with the behavior. In essence, you must stop listening. Connection to your heart and binge eating are incompatible states of being. A big part of recovery is learning to listen again, and act increasingly from a deeper, more peaceful, and, ultimately, far more powerful place.

▶ SECRETS

People work very hard to conceal a binge. I remember coming home after a date in high school, buying fast food, and eating it in the car, careful to hide the wrappers from my parents. My clients almost always have stories about stashes, about having forbidden foods hidden away for emergencies. It is a secretive behavior almost always because of the extraordinary shame associated with overeating, especially for people in larger bodies:

> I hide food everywhere. Cookies in my car, chocolate in the back of the desk drawer. I eat "perfectly" in front of people, always dieting. No one in my life has any idea I binge.

> No one knew about my binge days. I told people I was sick, or there was a family emergency. I spun some big tales to hide the truth.

As a result of such secrecy, binge eating is very isolating. Many of my clients talk about no one in their world knowing about the behavior, nor does anyone know about the emotional and cognitive turmoil that accompanies it:

> No one at work has any idea I'm sitting in weekly staff meetings obsessing about what to eat on my way home. I'm not even focused on what's happening. They would think I was crazy. After a binge, I won't see anyone for as long as I can. I feel like they can tell I've been doing it. They can see the shame right through me. I feel exposed and judged, even though it's all in my own head.

> I will put my binge evidence, food wrappers or food scraps underneath trash that's already in the garbage can. It's as much to keep it from my roommate as it is to keep it from myself.

Many talk about binge eating being a respite from a very critical inner voice. Shame messages about every perceived failure are temporarily silenced. There is a brief break before they come crashing in even worse, and the need to evade them begins anew.

> I simply go numb to my life, my thoughts, my feelings. If the phone rings, I am literally startled. I'm just not there.

> I can shut up body shame only when I eat.

> Binge eating shuts down memories of the past. It is the only time I really get away from them. Focusing on food just shuts them down.

Sometimes, when people feel significant social anxiety, a binge provides people a reason to refuse invitations, turn off the phone, and take a respite from worrying about what everybody thinks.

> When I binge, everything in my life gets suspended. I don't have to think about how I'm being seen, or who I may be disappointing.
>
> When I binge, I don't answer the phone or email. No one can get to me.

For people with limited tools and permission to set boundaries or express needs with others, binge eating is a primary method for allowing the psychological relief that comes from being alone.

For others, binge eating takes place in public, but still provides a way to deal with social fears.

> I am sitting across from friends, laughing and talking, and all the while I'm stuffing myself to the point of pain.
>
> It is a lot of work to be "on"; the food helps me get through. I can't say no to going out—because I might hurt somebody's feelings—so I go. My way of rewarding myself is to binge at dinner.
>
> It's right in front of my partner, but she has no idea that I'm bingeing. She doesn't know I have been eating all day.

▶ THE ROLE OF BODY AS ENEMY IN BED

In our culture, feeling bad about one's body is undoubtedly ubiquitous. Even more distressing, we take it as a given that feeling badly about at least some aspect of our appearance is *inherent*, as opposed to something learned. Psychologists have coined the term "normative discontent" to explain the idea that it becomes *normal* to feel some kind of shame or unhappiness because it is profoundly culturally common. Thus, while it may be anything but healthy or reasonable, such unhappiness or shame is considered normal. Without question, negative body image is a form of normative discontent. In one survey (Surrey, 1984), the number one wish of girls aged 11–17 who were told they had three magic wishes for anything they wanted was "to lose weight and keep it off." In another survey (Spettigue, 2004), middle-aged women were asked what they would most like to change about their lives, and more than half of them said their weight. Most every fashion magazine and talk show offer the latest weight loss strategies, and the gains and losses of Hollywood glitterati are constant grist for the gossip mills. Diet books are still bestsellers, and weight loss clinics are in most every strip mall. An entire industry has developed in the last decade offering a variety of surgical interventions all aimed at the holy grail of weight loss.

Not surprisingly then, negative body talk is part of the way many women connect and identify with each other. It becomes a normative part of conversation to berate our bodies. Such talk happens on social media, among coworkers at the proverbial water cooler, broadcast venomously on shows like *Real Housewives* and *Bridalplasty*, and in magazines like *Cosmopolitan*. All the public bashing makes personal body shaming seem completely *normal*. Additionally, and more insidious, the whole narrative is predicated on the idea that liking our physical appearance is yet another holy grail, something for which we are expected to strive throughout our lives. It is not a question in our minds about whether or not we actually want to devote time and energy to "look better." Of course we do; who wouldn't? It is virtually a moral imperative. Consider our reactions to those who have seemingly "let themselves go." We worry about their mental health, assuming at least some level of depression and a "giving up." And, perhaps, we might also feel just a touch of envy at their apparent freedom that we would never allow ourselves.

With such constant attack, our bodies become the prime targets for all that is wrong in our lives, for our fears, and for our anger.

> It is much easier for me to hate my body than to hate my boss. When I get mad at work, I focus on losing weight. Then I go home really upset about work, and I binge. Then I get up the next day and hate my body even more. My boss gets away with harassment and sexism, and my body pays. It's the most familiar, safest target of all.

We consider our bodies far more often as a billboard for the approval of others than assessing its needs as our earthly home. Many women (and increasing numbers of men) are in the process of fixing something about their bodies virtually all the time. Indeed, consider if anyone you know feels truly *at home* in their bodies, or at peace with how they look. How many of us see aging as beautiful? How many of us really notice the diversity of size and shape and color of the people around us without comparing them to a young, white, thin, able-bodied, fashionably dressed culturally decided "ideal"? How many people do you know who make decisions about their body's needs based on well-being or delight rather than appearance?

Given this paradigm, for most of us, food choices elicit guilt or pride. Working out is connected to deservedness of food—have we earned that pizza for dinner with enough minutes on the treadmill? Or better yet, can we eat something on the acceptable list and forego desire altogether? When people do feel better about their size or shape, it is almost always predicated on having lost weight or having made some significant change to their appearance. For many of my clients, the messages came early from seeing their parents' relationship with their own bodies:

> I remember being in fourth grade and my best friend told me she wore a girl's size 10. I was so excited because I thought I was a size 10 and now we were the same in my head. When I got home that day, I took my shirt off and saw a size 12. I was crushed.

> I was conscious, even as a little girl that my mother was embarrassed by her tummy (she had borne four children). She never seemed comfortable in her body. She told me that she always sucked in her stomach. I had no idea what that meant, but it was clearly an important part of being a woman.

In my own family, I recall the frequent quip "you can never be too rich or too thin." My colleague recalls hearing "nothing tastes as good as skinny feels." We have all been given extraordinary praise for losing weight. It often seems, based on the reactions of those around us, to be our greatest achievement. Given this, no need to wonder at the profound sense of shame when weight is almost inevitably regained.

▶ THE POWER OF FOOD

Food has extraordinary psychological power in our lives. It is literally our means to live, and one of the first ways we receive attention, care, and pleasure. It validates our right to exist, and tells us we have a place in the tribe in which we find ourselves. Although we do not always behave accordingly as a society, most of us believe access to good, plentiful, enjoyable food is a basic human right.

Throughout our lives, if we are fortunate to have access, food connects us to celebration, to our family heritage, our culture, and to significant times of transition and change. We may have foods that remind us of birthdays, specific relationships, and important places. When I taste a specific type of sugar cookie, I am back at my grandmother's house instantly. For my colleague, curry sends her memory immediately back to her aunt's kitchen. You may strongly remember your wedding cake or tomatoes from a garden. These can be simply pleasant sensations of nostalgia, but when an eating disorder exists, food memory associations are often far more complex.

Many foods have deep emotional charges; their taste and smell can trigger very powerful memories and somatic sensations. Certain foods can also be associated with different emotions.

> When I'm sad, I want ice cream. When I'm mad, I want potato chips.
> It's how my mom and I ate together. Early in recovery, it was the only
> way I was able to recognize my emotions.

Changing such powerful connections between food and feelings can seem impossible, especially when these foods still feel important.

> For me, it's a Dr Pepper every day. Because not having it feels weird.
> Feels untethered. Feels like I'm being good, because everyone knows
> soda is the root of evil. But I love Dr Pepper. It's part of me. It feels safe
> with my soda in hand. I know who I am.

When it has been scarce in a child's life, food comes to have a particular kind of power.

> Growing up with a single mom, we often didn't have much money,
> and sometimes we ran out of food. I would hide food just in case
> I needed it later. I spent my allowance on chocolate (instead of bus
> fare), and I stole candy from the drug store. I'd be really conservative
> with my stash, just eating a few bites here and there, until I couldn't
> stand the scarcity anymore. Then I'd eat it all. I'd feel such guilt
> because my sisters were still hungry. So I'd give them my treats for

a while. Then, slowly, I'd start hiding it all over again. I have never learned to eat in response to my body; it's either stash it and live with the hunger, or eat it all out of desperation and longing. With regard to food, I always feel either deprived or ashamed.

Recovery from BED requires us to closely examine this relationship with food from a vantage point of curiosity instead of judgment. Although we learned certain foods are good or bad, long-term recovery requires a profound change to this paradigm. When we do the work of healing, food increasingly becomes as it was in the beginning of life: sustenance, pleasure, and connection to life itself.

▶ THE "CURE" OF DIETING AND WEIGHT LOSS

Weight, shape and appearance are extraordinarily important in our culture's aesthetic ideal. Not only is appearance judged by size and shape; indeed, there is *moral* judgment. Thinner people are considered more disciplined, intelligent, and capable.

In addition, diet culture defines health in terms of thinness instead of fitness. One of the principles driving the $61 billion weight-loss-related industry is the notion that fat is *inherently* unhealthy. To be thin is best, no matter what a person must do to get there. However, a growing body of research challenges this paradigm. Does obesity actually *cause* ill health, result from it, both, or neither? Does weight loss (if it's even *possible*) lead to a longer, healthier life for most people? Are the methods for weight loss more costly to health than the weight? In fact, studies from the Centers for Disease Control and Prevention repeatedly find the lowest mortality rates among people whose body mass index puts them in the "overweight" and "mildly obese" categories. The largest epidemiological study ever conducted followed 1.8 million people over a 10-year follow-up period and demonstrated an inverted relationship between BMI and life expectancy, with the highest life expectancy in people with a BMI between 26 and 28 (in the "overweight" BMI category) and the lowest life expectancy in those with a BMI under 18 (in the "underweight" BMI category). Those with a BMI between 18 and 20 (in the "healthy weight" BMI category) had a lower life expectancy than those with a BMI between 34 and 36 (in the "obese" BMI category). And recent research suggests losing weight doesn't actually improve health biomarkers such as blood pressure, fasting glucose, or triglyceride levels over time for most people.

According to the dominant paradigm, thinner necessarily means healthier, and being healthy in many ways equates to being a better person. We moralize weight in our culture, and increasingly we moralize "health" as well. Good people are healthy people. In fact, current health statistics data tell us we cannot assume the nature of the impact of weight on health *for any given person*. If it is possible to be healthy and happy at many sizes and weights, however, that $61 billion dollar per year diet industry would have a tough time surviving. Body shame and blaming the victim would be much harder to sell.

Dieting is the most recommended strategy for this essential goal of weight control and it is a popular one. The Boston Medical Research Center reports approximately 45 million Americans diet each year. Surprisingly though, diets fail at an astonishing rate. This isn't breaking news. Doctors and researchers know the holy trinity of weight loss tools—diet, exercise, and medication—don't work. They also know yo-yo dieting is linked to, among other things, heart disease, insulin resistance, higher blood pressure, inflammation, and, ironically, long-term *weight gain*. Still, they push the same ineffective treatments, insisting they will make you not just thinner but healthier. In reality, 97 percent of dieters regain everything they lost, and then some, within 3 years. Your chance of keeping weight off for 5 years or more is about the same as your chance of surviving metastatic lung cancer: approximately 5 percent. Obesity research fails to reflect this truth, in part, because it rarely follows people for more than 18 months. This makes most weight loss studies disingenuous at best and downright deceptive at worst. Even some "anti-obesity" researchers acknowledge that weight losses will average 4–8 pounds after 2 to 4 years, and this is among educated, carefully selected, financially stable participants in diet trials. The expected loss is even less for people who are poor or uneducated (Katan, 2009). To add insult to this injury, dieters (regardless of life circumstances) always blame *themselves*, not dieting, for their virtually inevitable string of "failures."

Equating health to weight to moral fiber profoundly increases the shame around binge eating. While, as we have seen, there are many psychological and cultural factors at play in BED, we must also note that diet failure itself often plays a *causal* role in maintaining the cycle of binge eating. Dieting alone is not sufficient to *cause* binge eating disorder (many people diet and don't develop BED). In very specific ways, however, dieting contributes to the development and maintenance of BED.

Let's consider just two of the important biological processes that make dieting an ineffective and harmful strategy to stop binge eating. First and foremost, your body doesn't biologically know the difference between a diet and a famine. While one may be intentional and the other is clearly not, they both impact your *body* in the same way: an immediate threat to survival. Your body responds accordingly (and brilliantly). First, when you are hungry for a sustained period, your brain responds by literally making you think more about food. Study after study shows when we are hungry our thoughts turn naturally and unerringly to finding nourishment. In fact, research shows that your brain actually increases the reward value of foods in two ways: by making your taste buds take longer to reach the point of signaling satiety, and by reducing the release of fullness hormones while increasing the release of hunger hormones. Bottom line: humans are hard-wired to become obsessive about food when we are hungry, and to experience hunger more intensely. Thus, very high rates of weight regain on diets are not surprising; our body fights food restriction efforts at every turn. If it did not, we would not have survived as a species.

Second, our bodies do not like to change. If a particular behavior is connected to survival, our body resists changing it. Since adequate food intake and nutritional sustenance is required for survival, weight loss is perceived as a threat. In other words, our bodies strongly hang on to weight, and are most stable within a specific weight range. This is known as set point theory, and the evidence in its favor is compelling. According to this theory, our bodies, based on genetics, epigenetics, and our environment, have a weight range at which they are able to function optimally. Set point theory holds that one's body will fight to maintain that weight range if it is threatened. And, it will fight especially hard if there is weight *loss*, as opposed to weight *gain*. Once again, without this mechanism we would have been unlikely to survive. Thus, as such a threat (be it famine or diet) continues, the dieter's body becomes increasingly *efficient*. Weight loss becomes harder and harder to achieve—known as the dieter's plateau. In addition, weight is far more easily regained when the body is more efficient, even beyond set point weight. It is as though our body learns to *anticipate* famine in the future, and prepares accordingly.

Indeed, dieting proves to be the best way to *gain* weight (Field et al., 2003; Lowe et al., 2006). As we would suspect, research suggests dieters gain significantly more weight than nondieters (Neumark-Sztainer et al., 2012). For those with BED, this cycle can markedly increase the already powerful psychological drives to go to food with the hardwired protective mechanisms of the body itself. As a result of these impacts, recovery must address not only the psychological and cultural causes of BED, but also provide a whole new paradigm for how we understand food and make choices about how to best feed our bodies.

▶ THE WORK OF RECOVERY

Over the years, I have heard many of my clients who are far along in recovery actually find a kind of gratitude for their eating disorder. While they would certainly never *wish* for such a thing in their lives, there is a way the symptoms of binge eating and body hate brought them to questioning long-held beliefs about their bodies and themselves and to profound healing. This is not true for everyone with an eating disorder. For some people, adamant rejection of their eating disorder may be a critical part of long-term recovery. For many with BED, however, binge eating has been such a source of shame that to denigrate it further simply serves to compound the shame. It feels like yet another rejection—a denial of the struggle for change and a failure of willpower whenever they overeat. Since BED recovery is not black and white (as we will explore later), this setup is ineffective for long-term recovery. It is possible to have tremendous gratitude and compassion for the role food has played. In my personal and clinical experience, this kind of acceptance of, and compassion for, BED makes for the best chance at a peaceful relationship with food, body, and with self.

> Bingeing was a trail of breadcrumbs for me. I'm not sure how I would have had the drive to heal from my past without having something so distressing I had to confront.

> Without binge eating, I don't think I could have warned myself something big was missing from my life.

I know from my own journey that recovery allowed me to realize I could trust my body, feel the desire to protect it, and see it as my safe home in the world. BED recovery has provided such a way home for many of my clients, sometimes years in coming. As a result of doing the deeper work of recovery (and not simply seeking behavioral change), we increasingly choose living authentically in our bodies, and choose *connection* to our inner world over the disconnection sought from binge eating. We change our understanding of the world around us and our place in it. Thus, the journey toward healing goes forward.

The work of recovery from BED is in many ways an act of revolution. Until compassionate self-care and well-being is the ultimate goal (and available to all), recovery will not last. If your motivation for change is predicated on the need to "fix" what is wrong with your body, it is a motivation based in shame. As such, it will not allow you to truly hear your needs or be able to effectively address them. "We are the only species on earth capable of preventing our own flowering," wrote David Whyte. Shame is one of the primary reasons we so often get in our own way. Recovery should provide you with goals different than weight loss (which may or may not be possible long-term); it should provide you with a path for stepping into being authentic in the world. Recovery is, in many ways, about allowing our flowering to finally take place.

> To me, I define recovered as full freedom. The (food) choices I make aren't coming from fear or shame, but from authenticity. My choices are grounded in my body's wisdom.
>
> Once I glimpsed that all this fear about my body being wrong, about *me* being wrong, was coming from a young, scared part of me, I knew I could let my eating disorder, finally, go. It was all part of the same thing. It has all been about soothing fear; the binge eating and the shame were *both* part of surviving. Now I know I don't need to be afraid, and even when I am (which is a normal part of life), I can keep myself safe.

▶ COMING HOME: A NEW PATH

In an interview, a reporter once asked me to tell her in one sentence the most important thing to know about the deeper work of recovery from BED. From my experience, I can say it is essentially this: you must start at every level of your experience in the world to gently *listen* to yourself again. Recovery is the work of moving from safety based on conforming and disconnection, to safety based on turning *toward* ourselves.

Many of us who have experienced binge eating disorder learned fundamentally to keep away from our stories. We learned to feel fear or shame about what is closest to our heart, closest to the real truth of our authentic self. This reaction is a vestige of *survival*, not of *truth*. We should not feel shame or fear in connection to our own needs, but rather compassion and curiosity, and perhaps anger and frustration at the barriers we face. Recovery is very much about making our way back to such basic self-respect. "Recovery is going from an early life of lived vulnerability toward needs and desires, to believing we must disconnect from our self to be loved, to moving back to embracing and living in vulnerability," my clinical colleague Theresa Chesnut brilliantly suggests. Recovery often requires a 180-degree turn from what *feels* true in order to find what *is* true. With recovery work, the realization will come that you are actually *safest when you are in touch with yourself*, when you have compassionate access to your whole story, when you are in healthy relationships to others, and when you act from the desire to protect and cherish your life and your body, imperfections and all. As you increasingly make these changes, and learn to eat from an attuned sense of your body and from pleasure and permission, the desire to go to food slowly shifts. Urges come less and less often, and when they do come, you know how to turn *toward* the urge and deal with it effectively. You can increasingly learn to eat what you desire and stop when you are sated, trusting your body knows what to do. You can have a bump in the road and overeat or binge, but it remains only a *bump*; it does not turn into relapse. And you learn from it.

You also must learn that while the process of recovery is intensely personal, it is often a profoundly political act as well. To listen to your own body for the final say in what you need is in many ways an act of revolution toward the diet and body shame industry as a whole, and toward any cultural systems that reinforce oppression and reject inclusivity. Trusting your own body is a rejection of a dominant paradigm, one that makes billions of dollars from shame and rewards you for distrusting and disconnecting from your physical and psychological truths.

> Eventually, a new voice emerges, gradually, from within. She's on my side. She is me! "You can do this, honey," she says to herself. With deep breaths, staying attentive, saying no to the siren voices calling me to diet. It takes a lot of hard work, tears, compassion, and perseverance to discover, uncover, review, heal the brokenness that drives me to duck, hide, and binge away intolerable feelings. And to begin doing

things, a little at a time, that bring me joy, hope, love, gratefulness, openness, and peace.

▶ THE FIVE PRACTICES

When I began my recovery, I thought I knew myself. I knew what mattered to me, I knew my opinions and my strengths. I seemed self-assured to those around me. In truth, I was hiding most of my inner world from others and from myself. I looked successful and capable; inside, I was in an almost constant state of fear that the "rest of the story" might sneak out. I had had turbulent relationships with friends and family and little idea how to safely connect with others. I had no idea my binge eating was absolutely about this disconnection and loneliness. I also had no idea that the completely convincing shame-filled thoughts about these hidden parts of me were stories from long ago. I believed them not because they were *true*, but because they made sense at the time *given the world around me.* Recovery helped my thoughts, feelings, and body get unstuck from living in the past, and learn to live safely, with compassion for myself and others, in the present.

Recovery asks us to discover just how powerful we truly are. "Perhaps all the dragons in our lives are princesses who are only waiting to see us act just once with beauty and courage," the poet Rilke wrote (2013). Tenderness in recognizing our hungers, meeting them as we are able, fighting back when they are denied, and learning we can be safe even in vulnerability is what truly sustains recovery.

In my own healing, and in my work with clients, I have found five fundamental practices critical to long-term recovery from BED. These are not "steps" that we take and complete. Much like mastering playing the guitar or learning to write poetry, these are *processes*. We continue to hone and build as with any art, becoming better musicians or poets over time.

The Five Practices of Recovery are as follows:

1. Honor the impact of history

2. Meet binge urges with POWR

3. Escape the mythology of "thin"

4. Take back your body as your home

5. Build resiliency for long-term recovery

The Five Practices build on and reinforce each other over time. They are interdependent, working together to help us hear ourselves over the din of damaging messages, both internal and external. In the coming chapters, we will explore the practices one by one and consider how to implement each. Every person's inner language of recovery is different, and as such what works best is different, too.

It is imperative to remember this book is *not* treatment, but only a supplement and a support. Recovery, as with any other eating disorder, very often requires a psychotherapist with expertise in BED treatment. This is especially true if you are healing from trauma, dealing with significant mood disorders, or struggling with any kind of co-occurring addiction. Sometimes BED treatment requires a team of support people, including nutrition and medical professionals. Adjunct treatments such as art therapy, somatic therapies, equine therapy, and dance/movement therapies can be profoundly healing when informed with a BED-sensitive approach. Also remember a book is necessarily linear—recovery is not. Please keep in mind the Five Practices build on each other. Sometimes you will be far more focused on one area, less on another. The overall journey leads to living in your body with far more acceptance and peace.

Good news: recovery is possible. It is not perfect, we cannot be in control of all that impacts it, and is it never "finished." You continue to grow and heal, and come increasingly to know it is within the struggle that your gold lies.

> Today was a hard day. I felt so incredibly human and raw and emotional, and I couldn't be more grateful. There is nothing wrong with me. My body is not an apology. My body will not betray me. I am whole and flawed and important. I am thankful for every teacher and lesson and growing pain. I feel better. I feel my feelings better. Every day. I will never be perfect but I will always be enough. I will always be exactly where I'm supposed to be.

And so, with hope, gentleness, and the Five Practices, we move forward, heading home.

▶ BIBLIOGRAPHY

Bacon, L. (2010). *Health at every size: The surprising truth about your weight.* Dallas, TX: BenBella Books.

Becker, D. F., & Grilo, C. M. (2011). Childhood maltreatment in women with binge-eating disorder: Associations with psychiatric comorbidity, psychological functioning, and eating pathology. *Eating and Weight Disorders, 16*(2), e113–e120.

Berge, J. M., Didericksen, K., Bucchianeri, M., Prasad, S., & Neumark-Sztainer, D. (2016). Partnering with adolescents, parents, researchers, and family medicine clinics to address adolescent weight and weight-related behaviors. In M. R. Korin (Ed.), *Health promotion for children and adolescents* (pp. 309–324). New York, NY: Springer. Retrieved from http://doi.org/10.1007/978-1-4899-7711-3_15.

Bishop, E. (2010). *Innate temperament and eating disorder treatment.* Retrieved from www.addictionpro.com/article/innate-temperament-and-eating-disorder-treatment.

Borowsky, H. M., Eisenberg, M. E., Bucchianeri, M. M., Piran, N., & Neumark-Sztainer, D. (2016). Feminist identity, body image, and disordered eating. *Eating Disorders: The Journal of Treatment & Prevention, 24,* 297–311. Retrieved from http://doi.org/10.1080/10640266.2015.1123986.

Boston Medical Center. (n.d.). *An estimated 45 million Americans go on a diet each year.* Retrieved from www.bmc.org/nutrition-and-weight-management/weight-management.

Brach, T. (2004). *Radical acceptance: Embracing your life with the heart of a Buddha.* New York, NY: Bantam.

Brann, A. (2014). *Neuroscience for coaches.* London: Kogan Page.

Briere, J., & Scott, C. (2012). *Principles of trauma therapy: A guide to symptoms, evaluation, and treatment.* Thousand Oaks, CA: Sage Publications.

Bucchianeri, M. M., Gower, A. L., McMorris, B. J., & Eisenberg, M. E. (2016). Youth experiences with multiple types of prejudice-based harassment. *Journal of Adolescence, 51,* 68–75. Retrieved from http://doi.org/10.1016/j.adolescence.2016.05.012.

Courtois, C. A., Ford, J. D., & Herman, J. L. (2009). *Treating complex traumatic stress disorders: An evidence-based guide.* New York, NY: The Guilford Press.

Davis, C., & Katzman, M. A. (1999). Perfection as acculturation: Psychological correlates of eating problems in Chinese male and female students living in the United States. *International Journal of Eating Disorders, 25*(1), 65–70.

Feldman, M. B., & Meyer, I. H. (2007). Eating disorders in diverse lesbian, gay, and bisexual populations. *International Journal of Eating Disorders, 40*, 218–226. Retrieved from http://doi.org/10.1002/eat.20360.

Field, A. E., Austin, S. B., Taylor, C. B., Malspies, S., Rosner, B., Rockett, H. R., . . . Colditz, G. A. (2003). Relation between dieting and weight change among pre-adolescents and adolescents. *Pediatrics, 112*, 900–906.

French, S. A., Story, M., Neumark-Sztainer, D., Downes, B., Resnick, M., & Blum, R. (1997). Ethnic differences in psychosocial and health behavior correlates of dieting, purging, and binge eating in a population-based sample of adolescent females. *International Journal of Eating Disorders, 23*(3), 315–322. Retrieved from http://doi.org/10.1002/(SICI)1098-108X(199711)22:3<315::AID-EAT11>3.0.CO;2-X.

Gearhardt, A. N., Roberto, C. A., Seamans, M. J., Corbin, W. R., & Brownell, K. D. (2009). Preliminary validation of the Yale food addiction scale. *Appetite, 52*, 430–436. Retrieved from http://doi.org/10.1016/j.eatbeh.2013.07.002.

Goeree, M. S., Ham, J. C., & Daniela, I. (2011). *Race, social class, and bulimia nervosa.* IZA Discussion Paper No. 5823. Retrieved from http://ftp.iza.org/dp5823.pdf.

Grilo, C. M., Masheb, R. M., Brody, M., Toth, C., Burke-Martindale, C. H., & Rothschild, B. S. (2005). Childhood maltreatment in extremely obese male and female bariatric surgery candidates. *Obesity Research, 13*(1), 123–130.

Herrin, M., & Matsumoto, N. (2011, March). The truth about so called sugar addiction. In E. Triboli & E. Resch (Eds.), *Eating Disorder News.* IntuitiveEating.org as retrieved from www.intuitiveeating.org/category/binge-eating/.

Hudson, J. I., Hiripi, E., Pope, H. G. Jr., & Kessler, R. C. (2007). The prevalence and correlates of eating disorders in the National Comorbidity Survey Replication. *Biological Psychiatry, 61*(3), 348–358. Retrieved from http://doi.org/10.1016/j.biopsych.2.

Katan, M. B. (2009). Weight-loss diets for the prevention and treatment of obesity. *New England Journal of Medicine, 360*, 923–925. Retrieved from http://doi.org/10.1056/NEJMe0810291

Kilbourne, J. (1994). Still killing us softly: Advertising and the obsession with thinness. In P. Fallon, M. Katzman, & S. Wooley (Eds.), *Feminist perspectives on eating disorders* (pp. 395–419). New York, NY: The Guilford Press.

Kristeller, J. L., & Wolever, R. Q. (2011). Mindfulness-based eating awareness training for treating binge eating disorder: The conceptual foundation. *Eating Disorders: The Journal of Treatment & Prevention, 19*(1), 49–61. Retrieved from http://doi.org/10.1080/10640266.2011.533605.

Lowe, M. R., Annunziato, R. A., Markowitz, J. T., Didie, E., Bellace, D. L., Riddell, L., . . . Stice, E. (2006). Multiple types of dieting prospectively predict weight gain during the freshman year of college. *Appetite, 47*, 83–90.

Marques, L., Alegria, M., Becker, A. E., Chen, C., Fang, A., Chosak, A., & Diniz, J. B. (2011). Comparative prevalence, correlates of impairment, and service utilization for eating disorders across U.S. ethnic groups: Implications for reducing ethnic disparities in health care access for eating disorders. *The International Journal of Eating Disorders, 44*(5), 412–420. doi.org/10.1002/eat.20787.

Mitchison, D., Hay, P., Slewa-Younan, S., & Mond, J. (2014). The changing demographic profile of eating disorder behaviors in the community. *BMC Public Health, 14*(1). Retrieved from http://doi.org/10.1186/1471-2458-14-943.

Müller, M. J., Bosy-Westphal, A., & Heymsfield, S. B. (2010, August 9). Is there evidence for a set point that regulates human body weight? *PF1000 Medicine Reports, 2*, 59. Retrieved from http://doi.org/10.3410/M2-59.

Neumark-Sztainer, D. R., Wall, M., Story, M., & Standish, A. R. (2012). Dieting and unhealthy weight control behaviors during adolescence: Associations with 10-year changes in body mass index. *Journal of Adolescent Health, 50*, 80–86. http://doi.org/10.1016/j.jadohealth.2011.05.010.

Oliver-Pyatt, W. (2003). *Fed up!* New York, NY: McGraw-Hill.

Reagan, P., & Hersch, J. (2005). Influence of race, gender, and socioeconomic status on binge eating frequency in a population-based sample. *International Journal of Eating Disorders, 38*(3), 252–256. Retrieved from http://doi.org/10.1002/eat.20177.

Rilke, R. M. (2013). *Letters to a young poet.* New York, NY: Penguin Classics.

Sanlier, N., Yassibas, E., Bilici, S., Sahin, G., & Celik, B. (2016). Does the rise in eating disorders lead to increasing risk of orthorexia nervosa? Correlations with gender, education, and body mass index. *Ecology of Food and Nutrition, 55*, 266–278. Retrieved from http://doi.org/10.1080/03670244.2016.1150276.

Spettigue, W. & Henderson, K. (2004). Eating disorder and the role of the media. *Canadian Child and Adolescent Psychiatry Review, 13*(1), 16–19.

Spurrell, E. B., Wilfley, D. E., Tanofsky, M. B., & Brownell, K. D. (1997). Age of onset for binge eating: Are there different pathways to binge eating? *International Journal of Eating Disorders, 21*(1), 55–65. Retrieved from http://dx.doi.org/10.1002/(SICI)1098-108X(199701)21:1<55::AID-EAT7>3.0.CO;2-2.

Stepanikova, I., Baker, E. H., Simoni, Z. R., Zhu, A., Rutland, S. B., Sims, M., & Wilkinson, L. L. (2017). The role of perceived discrimination in obesity among African Americans. *American Journal of Preventative Medicine, 52*(1), Supplement 1, S77–S85. Retrieved from http://doi.org/10.1016/j.amepre.2016.07.034.

Stice, E., & Bohon, C. (2012). Eating disorders. In T. Beauchaine & S. Linshaw (Eds.), *Child and adolescent psychopathology* (2nd Ed.). New York, NY: Wiley.

Stice, E., Marti, C. N., Shaw, H., & Jaconis, M. (2010). An 8-year longitudinal study of the natural history of threshold, subthreshold, and partial eating disorders from a community sample of adolescents. *Journal of Abnormal Psychology, 118*(3), 587–597. Retrieved from http://doi.org/10.1037/a0016481.

Surrey, J. (1991). Eating patterns as a reflection of women's development. In J. V. Jordan, A. G. Kaplan, I. P. Stiver, J. L. Surrey, & J. Baker Miller (Eds.). *Women's growth in connection: Writings from the stone center.* New York, NY: The Guilford Press.

Walker, P. (2013). *Complex PTSD from surviving to thriving: A guide and map for recovering from childhood trauma.* Charleston, SC: CreateSpace Independent Publishing Platform.

Ware, B. (2012). *The top five regrets of the dying: A life transformed by the dearly departing.* Carlsbad, CA: Hay House.

Westerberg, D. P., & Waitz, M. (2013). Binge-eating disorder. *Osteopathic Family Physician, 5*(6), 230–233. Retrieved from http://doi.org/10.1016/j.osfp.2013.06.003.

Westwater, M. L. (2016). "Sugar addiction: The state of the science." *European Journal of Nutrition.* November 10, 55–69.

Whyte, D. *We are the only species on earth capable of preventing our own flowering.* Retrieved from http://quoteaddicts.com/836520.

2

How BED Happens and Why It Makes Sense

Moving Forward by Healing the Past

"Chev, come downstairs please. Dad and I want to speak with you."

"Why? What do you want?"

"Just get down here," Mom yelled.

My day had begun with piano lessons across town. A hot June day, my brother and I stopped at RubinsonsGeneral Store on the walk home. I looked forward to this weekly opportunity to buy candy bars. Shortly after moving in to the old Victorian-era house a year ago, I discovered a loose floorboard in my bedroom. When I lifted it, I found a small wooden box built between the joists—a place to hide valuables. For me, it was the place I hid my shame.

When my brother and I arrived home from piano lessons, I noticed Dad's car in the driveway, which was unusual for noon on a Tuesday. I ran quickly upstairs to my room, lifted the floorboard, and shoved the candy bars into the box. That's when I heard Mom call me downstairs.

"Take a seat," she told me. Mom lay sprawled on the blue floral Victorian neoclassic style couch and Dad, smoking his pipe, sat legs crossed on the high-back chair across the living room. I walked past the mirror between the two windows and glanced at myself. Quickly, I turned away and sat in the high back chair next to Dad. I did not want my parents to know the type of distress I felt looking in a mirror.

"We want to talk to you about something and please know it's because we love you and want the best for you," Mom began.

"Mom found the stash of goodies in your room and we need to talk about this," Dad continued.

My heart began to pound, and I wanted to shrink into a corner.

"Chev, please don't cry," Mom said.

Tears began to roll down my cheeks while the prickly sensation of shame shot through every part of my body. I began to feel oddly bloated, as if my body were expanding and taking up the entire room.

"I was an overweight kid and I know if we don't do something now it may be too late," Mom said. "Dad and I have an idea." Mom said Weight Watchers has camps for kids my age and they thought the program might be helpful.

"*I will never go to a fat camp!*" I screamed. "I'm already trying to diet and will do it on my own. I don't need a bunch of people telling me how to eat."

"We need to do something Chevese. We cannot continue like this. This is not normal and it's not healthy."

Mom was right. More than anything, I wanted to be thin. I wanted to wear the clothes the girls in my seventh grade class would wear this fall when school began. I wanted to be liked by boys and I wanted my parents to be proud of me.

"Why don't I make an appointment with the doctor and we can talk to him about it," Mom suggested. I agreed, despite the worry he would be angry with me because I did not follow the diet he gave me the last visit.

The pit in my stomach began first thing in the morning on the day of my doctor's appointment and continued throughout the day. I kept hoping that when I stepped on the scale in Dr. Knepper's office I would be several pounds lighter. I worked hard to diet since the conversation with Mom and Dad about my weight. I skipped breakfast, no snacks, and kept my meals to one helping. Hunger gnawed at me all the time, but I did everything I could to ignore it. I checked how I looked in the mirror all the time, too. If my stomach kept getting flatter, then I would be motivated to keep going.

Mom picked me up after school and I said barely a word to her in the car. The doctor's visit began with the nurse taking my height and weight.

"It looks like you have gained 3 pounds since your last visit," she said in a matter-of-fact tone.

I turned around to look at Mom but she had already walked down the hall to the examination room. I followed her and sat down on a hard, plastic chair to wait for the doctor. An awkward silence sat between us. I understood she genuinely worried about me. I also knew there was something beyond how much I ate and what I weighed that made this difficult for Mom. I wanted to somehow lessen her worry. At the time, I could not conceive she struggled with an eating disorder that would remain hidden for decades, nor how closely I followed in her footsteps.

Dr. Knepper came in to the examination room and reviewed my charts.

"Are you ready to lose weight?" he asked me. "Are you willing to help her?" he asked Mom.

"Of course!" we both answered.

After a quick examination and some questions, he sat down on his wheeled chair and scooted it toward me. He put both hands on my knees and looked directly in to my eyes. I felt increasingly uncomfortable, but held his gaze. "Chevese, we are going to nip this problem in the bud. You want to be thin, right?"

"Yes." I answered. Why was he asking me this question? Of course I want to be thin. Who in their right mind would want to be fat?

"Great, then are you willing to follow my directions exactly as I give them to you?" He looked directly in to my eyes.

"Yes," I said again and nodded my head.

Excellent! Hold tight, I'll be right back.

As he left the room, I felt a wave of calm come over me and I looked at my mom. She and I were both smiling, and I knew she felt the same confidence in whatever solution the doctor would recommend.

The doctor came back in to the room with a small white envelope and a stack of papers. He sat on his wheeled stool and scooted once again to my side. He turned the front of the envelope toward me, so I could see the directions he wrote in his illegible handwriting.

"You will take one of these pills in the morning before breakfast and another in the evening before dinner. They will help curb your appetite, so you will eat less, and it is very important that you remember to take them every day. This will significantly cut the number of calories you consume daily and we should see the fat melt away," he explained.

I could not believe it was this easy. A small pill twice a day and I could finally wear the clothes I wanted and the boy on whom I had a major crush would see me in a whole new light. As an added benefit, I would no longer be teased about my weight or the last in my class picked for teams during gym class.

Two weeks later, I would find myself involuntarily vomiting at a friend's house after bingeing on food that I stole from the kitchen in the night.

Earlier that evening, I decided not to take my diet pill and ate dinner after barely eating for days. The pizza and chips tasted better than any food I remembered, and I could think of nothing else for the remainder of the evening. I knew if I did not find more food, I would not be able to sleep. My mind focused on food and I did not enjoy the usual sleepover activities. I told my friend I did not feel good and needed to go to bed. Once I was sure the household was asleep, I snuck in to the kitchen and ate an entire box of ice cream bars.

Within minutes of crawling back in to my sleeping bag, I could feel my mouth begin to water and my stomach rumble. I ran to the bathroom just in time for my binge to make its way into the toilet. I sat on the floor and cried. I was 12, but wanted my mom to be there to comfort me as she always did when I was sick. No one was there for me that night and I felt lonely and ashamed.

I carefully put the wrappers in a plastic bag and hid it in my suitcase. I hoped no one would notice the ice cream bars were gone in the morning. With some distance between the night's events and the morning, I felt relief in that my body chose to get rid of the pizza and ice cream. It was terrible to be alone and vomiting, but the upside was getting rid of all the calories I consumed the evening before.

I was on my way to being thin. Life was definitely improving.

▶ THE PAST MATTERS

When I initially went into therapy, I was looking only for behavior change. I needed tips and strategies for addressing my binge behaviors. I truly did not link my past experiences in the world, or my resulting relationships with myself and others, as important to the process of change. I now know just how much I had to change to let go of binge eating. I had to learn I was enough *as is*, and that others could care about the real me. I needed to discover that binge eating was a way to disconnect from loneliness, anger, shame, and fear, and it was something I didn't need anymore. I needed to hear, and use, my voice for protection of myself and to advocate for change around me. The journey has looked nothing like I expected.

▶ NATURAL PRESENCE

Life begins for all of us with inherent trust in our body. Needs and desires exist without judgment; our body is simply our experiential home. We are dependent on our caretakers, looking to them for survival every minute of every day. We express to them our hunger, need for touch, for sleep, and for connection. We slowly learn which behaviors are acceptable and which are not. Emotions are brief, experienced fully, and dissipate quickly when we are in a stable enough environment and our needs are basically met. We learn through being heard and tended that the world and others are safe enough and that danger, always a part of life, does pass.

As children, we truly inhabit our physical bodies. Instead of a focus on how it appears, we *experience* our physical selves as a source of information about the world and our needs in it. If we are fed and clothed and touched lovingly, we navigate the world with body trust and integrity.

▶ LIFE BEFORE SHAME

Early in life, our world is largely determined by the psychological and physical health of our primary caregivers. If they are consistently available, willing and able to parent, and psychologically healthy, we will do well. If we have healthy genes, resources (including adequate food, health care, and shelter), and enough time spent with important others, we feel the world to be safe and are able to experience our needs and feelings with minimal censorship. Over time, when we encounter fear, we learn to listen to it effectively without being overwhelmed by it. We learn to navigate the world and challenge that which is damaging or dangerous. When something feels bad—physically or psychologically—we address the issue directly or get away from the danger as the situation warrants. We learn to trust our inner experience as a reliable truth teller and act on it accordingly from increasing wisdom. When others hurt or anger us, we believe we can say so without fear of retribution or loss of connection.

Feeling heard and being believed is critical for children as they develop in order to trust their own experiences and to feel loved by others. When our caregivers handle our feelings effectively *most* of the time, we flourish. No caregiver does this perfectly. Perfection would be both impossible and ineffective; we need to learn to cope when our needs are not met or our desires go unfulfilled. We have to learn patience, how to deal with loss and disappointment, and discover that love can survive conflict.

We must learn to balance our own needs with the needs of others, knowing we are safe and accepted even when a need goes unmet. If caretakers are healthy and emotionally available most of the time, they help us develop our own inner ability to self-soothe in times of distress. We become resilient, able to handle threat, loss, disappointment, and unmet desire. Over time, we learn how to identify and name feelings and needs without judgment, and feel compassion for others and ourselves. Indeed, feeling compassion and empathy is a natural state when basic needs are met. Helping others feels good and natural, but is balanced with caring for our own needs. And when we feel fear, as we naturally are wired to do, we can attend to it, respond to any real dangers, and not be consumed with anxiety, dread, or hopelessness.

When we have safe support from caregivers, we learn to be in relationships effectively. We learn boundaries, to use our inside voice, to wait our turn, to realize others see things differently. The dance between self and other is navigable, even if sometimes bumpy or unpredictable. We learn how to recognize relationships that are not good for us. We stay checked in to our own experience, and are at home in our own bodies. We handle what comes our way, ask for support without guilt when we need it, and offer compassion to others and to ourselves. We can struggle and suffer and fall down and get back up, feel joy and pain and excitement and grief. In other words, we navigate our messy, imperfect life without toxic shame or fear, or a driving need to numb our inner world.

▶ THE LOSS OF THE WORLD

For people struggling with binge eating disorder, things are often quite different. For many with BED, relationships have often offered limited security and may bring exposure to physical or emotional harm, and the risk of being harshly judged. Critical to development, being seen and validated is scarce. As Brené Brown (2012) writes,

> A deep sense of love and belonging is an irreducible need of all people. We are biologically, cognitively, physically, and spiritually wired to love, to be loved, and to belong. When those needs are not met, we don't function as we were meant to. We break. We fall apart. We numb. We ache. We hurt others. We get sick.

And we develop coping strategies like binge eating. Bingeing becomes a strategy to cope with fear, shame, anger, and loss. It may provide a way to "start over" with a clean slate, the shame somehow cleansed.

> I have to eat the rest of a binge food once I start because I blew it. I have to get out of the shame of having ruined my diet by eating all that is left. It does not make rational sense, but emotionally it staves off the incredible shame I feel for having eating these foods at all. I can't stand eating *some* of a forbidden food; I have to get rid of it all, and then start over again fresh.

When others are both essential to our safety *and* dangerous psychologically or physically, we are caught in a paradox. The very people we need most are also most able to harm our development and sense of self. We become afraid of making mistakes and failing to meet expectations.

> As the eldest child, I cared for all the younger siblings. There was no place for me to be little, or to need help. Food was a place to stop being in charge. I could just be out of control, at last.

Life with such fear is an extraordinary amount of work, a burdensome weight. And while humans can adapt to even the most chaotic environments, such adaptation exacts a price. A lack of safety or approval from caregivers renders us vulnerable to messages of shame from all directions as we mature. By adulthood, with such messages firmly entrenched, we are vulnerable to a cacophony of negative internal judgments, able to be triggered by the smallest transgression from perfection. An omission of an important point during a presentation, arriving late to meet a friend for coffee, or an unflattering photo can all be traps for obsessive thinking, keeping shameful feelings fueled for days or even years.

Brené Brown (2012) defines shame as the "intensely painful feeling or experience of believing that we are flawed and therefore unworthy of love and belonging—something we've experienced, done, or failed to do makes us unworthy of connection." Shame is different than guilt. We feel guilty about an inappropriate *action*. Guilt is powerful, but its influence can be positive, keeping us from harming others and endangering the social fabric of communities. Shame is different. It erodes courage and causes us to disengage. It functions to keep us in line with the real or perceived expectation of others when those expectations may not fit with our authentic self or our needs. While shame might help keep us in the good graces of caretakers, *it hurts because it is not truth, and it limits our very experience of life.* When unexamined and unhealed, the impact of shame, especially if consistently felt, is profound enough to drive and sustain many damaging attempts at coping, including binge eating disorder.

When the need to be loved and the need to be authentic are regularly at odds over time, the results are often psychologically catastrophic. When a conflict occurs in childhood with caretakers, we *must put their wishes first*; there is no option. The choosing is not conscious or considered.

> My mother's depression was up to me to fix. I read to her. I put cream on her hands. I brushed her hair. When she stayed sad, I tried even harder. I could never leave her; I was terrified she wouldn't be OK without my help.

As a result of this "de-selfing," parts of us remain underdeveloped. At the same time, other parts overdevelop in an effort to meet others' expectations and conditions for acceptance. These adaptations are common in the development of binge eating disorder. Many of my clients feel like old souls in certain areas of their lives, and like small children in others.

> I run an entire company, paying attention to every last detail. But I can't tell my best friend when I'm hurt by something she said, or tell my partner when I'm afraid. Either I just don't know that's how I feel in the moment, or if I do, I feel too vulnerable or ashamed to say it out loud. I just obsess about it until I need to block it out.

We learn, through punishment, neglect, judgment, and conditional love that parts of us are simply not acceptable. In families where BED develops, feelings in general are often minimized, debated, or avoided. Anger, fear, joy, grief, shame, or any other emotions are not welcomed by the most important people in our world.

> Being sad was considered a waste of time in my family. I was told to carry on after big losses. I would just hide my tears, and feel embarrassed for being so weak.

> Every time I was angry, I was told nice girls don't get mad. I felt even angrier, and then really, really embarrassed that I'd let my feeling get the better of me.

> I am half Korean and half Japanese. I learned never to talk about my Korean side to my traditional Japanese grandparents. It was bad enough in their mind that I was fat and unmarried, according to my mother. I had enough bad things about me, so I should at least work harder to lose weight and get married.

We learn parts of our most basic self must be altered or hidden and that there is *something intrinsically wrong with our feelings.* If they begin to surface, a loud inner critical voice and somatic sensations of shame shut our authentic responses down. We learn to discredit and ignore significant parts of our lived experience. This shame and fear is at the root of the most toxic stories of childhood, narratives we may still largely live by, unedited and unexamined.

> I always knew I was gay. Anything my father associated with gayness was not OK. I learned to stuff anything and everything that he'd think was wimpy. No silliness, no tears, no sadness at all. I tried to be like him instead of like me.

For many with BED, anxiety comes to feel like a *normal state*. Being worried feels like the nature of reality itself. We develop what Buddhists call "monkey mind," constantly assessing where we might next make a mistake, disappoint those we need most, and end up alone.

> [Life is] about worrying. All the time. It's imagining conversations where I excuse, defend, justify myself. Preparing for accusations, criticism, and judgment. It's exhausting.

> The number one reason I binge is to avoid the experience of fear of screwing up.

> I am constantly going over what I did wrong, might do wrong, will do wrong in the future. It might be being fat. It might be being loud. It might be basically anything. Growing up, it could have been anything, at any point. It just feels like reality to be afraid.

We are supposed to move toward others when we feel unsafe or insecure, feeling the validation of being loved regardless of imperfections or mistakes. But, when connection and validation have been elusive or dangerous, we do the opposite: we *disconnect* from others. Fear of others' judgment becomes a way of life, driving us further away from social engagement. We become fixated on looking for danger, anticipating it in every relationship. Inner critical voices go unchallenged, and are even more powerful and convincing. Soothing with food becomes a valuable survival strategy.

> Relationships feel like a sheer cliff, or a tsunami. They could shatter at any point. I am alone in this life. And ill-equipped to be safe.

Disconnection from others leaves few options for soothing troubling thoughts and feelings. Food is often the safest path out of feeling overwhelmed. And this very act, while calming in the moment, keeps fear and shame at toxic levels in the long run. The cycle repeats, and it seems impossible to escape.

▶ A NOTE ABOUT BLAME

When examining personal and family history, it is important to remember that *the goal is not to blame family members*. It is to tell the truth of lived experience, and honor the impact of the past on our present life. It is imperative to understand the *why* behind our relationships with food in order to understand and allow our feelings and needs, and build the self-compassion necessary to heal long term. We need to be able to offer ourselves understanding for our adaptations to adversity (including binge eating). It is not effective to simply "keep calm and carry on," or to focus only on the *symptom* of binge eating. We need to understand the impact of the past. We need not live there, or dwell in it. But we must not minimize or deny it, either. Particularly for those who have experienced trauma and loss, our current physical and emotional experience of the world is fundamentally altered by an unresolved past. Without doing the deeper work, recovery cannot be sustained.

It is exceptionally rare that parents or other primary caregivers *set out* to harm a child. Mostly caregivers do the best they are able. They, too, are products of a culture of weight discrimination, body shame, myriad oppressions, and sometimes, their own eating disorders. Additionally, caregivers who abuse or exploit a child often do so in response to their own perceived inadequacies or history of unresolved fear and shame. While this in no way excuses the behavior, it does speak to the legacy of these dynamics across generations. The cycle stops only when truth is acknowledged and addressed. We might consider thinking here about the critical difference between intention and impact. While caregivers may not *intend* harm, the *impact* of their behavior may be a different story entirely. Both truths need to be honored if we are to move forward.

Our environment plays an enormous role in the development of BED, but so do some things that may well be a function of our physiology. The intensity with which we experience emotion, our intelligence, and level of introversion, for example, may be in part determined by the interaction of genetic factors and neurochemistry. How genes are expressed is largely a function of environmental factors; it is the combination of these influences that makes us who we are. The work of recovery is simply to tell the truth about our own experience from a place of compassion and gentleness. For many, this change is an act of revolution.

▶ WHEN SAFETY IS SCARCE

When we talk about trauma, most people think of what is referred to as "single incident trauma." This refers to the impact of discreet, often singular events such as natural disasters, war, accidents, or witnessing harm done to others. While this is definitely a form of trauma, the clinical definition is broader and more nuanced.

Whether or not an event will be experienced as traumatic depends on a number of factors, including the level of support available following the experience, the meaning ascribed to the event and its aftermath, and the age and maturity of the survivor. When our *relationships* are the source of such danger in early life, human brains develop differently to adapt to the situation. This can result in something referred to as "complex trauma," and people with such histories are especially susceptible to disorders like BED. By definition, complex trauma is caused by the impact of direct harm, exploitation, or maltreatment, either chronic or erratic, including neglect (emotional or physical), abandonment by or significant lack of access to caregivers, or aversion to the child by primary caregivers or other ostensibly responsible adults. Complex trauma exists on a spectrum, and impacts people differently. When such experiences are inescapable, sufficiently distressing, and repeated over time, the impact on identity and sense of safety is immense and enduring.

Complex trauma is common in our country. Currently one in six children in the U.S. is living in an abusive situation. This amounts to approximately 12 million children, and does not include families in which the damage done is primarily in the form of psychological shaming. Of all eating and related disorders, BED has the highest correlation with complex trauma. In a recent research overview on BED and childhood experiences, a total of 59 percent of BED patients reported emotional abuse, 36 percent reported physical abuse, 30 percent reported sexual abuse, 69 percent reported emotional neglect, and 49 percent reported physical neglect. According to Brewerton (2007), 74 percent of 293 women attending residential eating disorder treatment with binge behavior indicated they had experienced significant trauma, and 52 percent reported symptoms consistent with a diagnosis of PTSD. In one study (van der Kolk, Perry, & Herman, 1991), 50 percent of patients with trauma developed binge behaviors. Symptoms of complex trauma are far less correlated with food restriction behaviors (about 15 percent). Twenty percent of the general population has experienced trauma, which, while disturbing, is far less than we see in those with binge behaviors. While some people develop binge behaviors in the absence of trauma, a significant portion of people dealing with the disorder report traumatic experiences. The act of binge eating, often impulse-driven and dissociative, can be a readily available means of coping for both children and adults.

Complex trauma, as noted above, is *interpersonal,* meaning it happens in the *relationship* between people with different levels of power. It often occurs at vulnerable times in the victim's life, especially in early childhood or adolescence, and may well continue into adult relationships. Different from other types of trauma, the *responsibility for these experiences is almost always internalized by the victim,* thus creating the narrative of being bad and deserving the abuse or maltreatment.

> I was five when my stepfather sexually abused me. I needed him in my life so badly, and my mom did too. We couldn't afford the rent without him. I remember clinging to him, begging him not to leave, despite what he did to me. I felt like a loser my whole life because I begged him to stay. What kind of freak wants their abuser to stay? What I didn't realize is that I was still shaming myself for what he did to me. He is still off the hook, and I'm always in the wrong. Now I know I had no other choice but to blame myself.

According to Christine A. Courtois (2010), interpersonal traumatization causes "a more severe reaction in the victim than does traumatization that is impersonal, the result of a random event or an "act of God," such as a disaster (i.e., a natural disaster such as a hurricane or tsunami, a technological disaster) or an accident (i.e., a motor vehicle or other transportation accident, a building collapse) due to its "deliberate" versus accidental causation. Worse yet, complex trauma-inducing experiences are often recurring and may become chronic. When this damage occurs at the hand of someone in an ongoing relationship with the child (i.e., parent or caregiver, other family member, clergy member, teacher, coach, babysitter, therapist), a sacred trust is breached; unless there is significant and effective action taken to address the experience, traumatization is likely.

A person who experiences early relational trauma may feel a persistent sadness about life, to the point sometimes of persistent suicidal thoughts. They may struggle with either explosive or inhibited anger. The person may have little or no conscious memory of what happened, or they may relive these events over and over in body or mind. Events may present in a sensible chronological order, or be fragmented and temporally disjointed.

Sometimes, survivors feel detached from their thoughts, feelings, or body sensations. Some may feel a chronic helplessness, shame, guilt, stigma, or an ongoing sense of being somehow different from others. They may struggle with a loss of faith, or a sense of hopelessness and despair, and may not even know why. Children so need to believe their parents love and care for them that they deny and minimize the most egregious neglect and abuse to protect the image of caregivers, and to protect some sense of safety and rationality in the world around them.

Despite such experiences, humans are incredibly resilient and able to endure profound hardship, especially at young ages. Children can recover from negative experiences provided there is adequate and age-appropriate support and information available, a safe environment is restored as soon as possible, and it is repeatedly made clear to the child that they are not to blame for what has happened. When this is not the case, however, such experiences often overwhelm a child's ability to cope. Children can be left fearing for their safety, or their worthiness for love and care. They may feel emotionally, cognitively, or physically overwhelmed by fear or shame or both. When such events happen very early in development, they may not be fully remembered or even describable with language by the survivor. They may instead be experienced somatically or emotionally, without a cogent accompanying narrative. This unfortunately makes many people doubt that things were "that bad." Even though they likely have a long-standing fear of connection, significant irrational shame, and very low self-worth, if survivors cannot tell their story clearly with words, they tend not to believe their own experience of reality. They often label themselves instead as weak or "too sensitive." Sadly, others may do so as well, misunderstanding the reasons for a survivor's possibly destructive behaviors.

▶ VERBAL AND EMOTIONAL ABUSE

Feeling cherished is essential to developing a healthy self for human beings. We need to know we are valued and heard in order to internalize healthy self worth and self compassion. Many of my BED clients have experienced significant verbal shaming and emotional neglect. However, they often diminish the psychologically crippling impact of venomous words or rejection of their emotions by caregivers. "He didn't mean it. It's just how he talks" or "I'm too sensitive" are common explanations for strong feelings about words and tone. Often, family members and other adults minimize the impact too, suggesting it's "not as bad" as other forms of abuse. Culturally and socially, we hold firmly to the narrative that verbal shaming is simply part of healthy badinage. "Slamming" each other with insults is a deeply rooted part of our collective humor; sarcasm is a much celebrated talent.

For many of my clients who have experienced verbal and emotional abuse as well as physical or sexual abuse, the harder work has been overcoming the haunting words, gestures of withdrawal, and emotional shaming from caregivers. Critical or hostile words and tone slowly but surely destroy self-esteem, replacing it with toxic internalized shame and self-criticism. Trauma specialist and clinician Pete Walker (2013) notes, "Growing up emotionally neglected is like nearly dying of thirst just outside the fenced off fountain of a parent's kindness and interest. Emotional neglect makes children feel worthless, unlovable and excruciatingly empty, with a hunger that gnaws deeply at the center of their being, leaving them starving for human warmth and comfort—a hunger that often morphs over time into an insatiable appetite for substances and/or addictive processes."

> My parents were comfortable assigning chores, but no instruction or support was ever provided to ensure successful completion. I tried, and from my 7-year-old perspective, thought I did what was asked. Until I was yanked out of my sleep and bed at 1 a.m. to look at the "half-assed job" I did putting away the silverware. Did I put it in the wrong drawer? I was sure I hadn't. I looked at my Dad, confused, which seemed to infuriate him further. "Look!" he said. I looked, still unsure what the problem was. Then, he pointed it out. I had placed the spoons in their slot in the silverware drawer, but I had not put them in so they were nesting against each other. They were willy-nilly backwards and forwards, and not spooning against each other the way my Dad thought they should be.
>
> I heard all the time "How could you not know that? How can you be this stupid?" I can't remember ever feeling like I was capable of doing a good job of anything.
>
> To this day, when I talk about my feelings, I hear a voice tell me I'm whining and being a silly girl.
>
> I remember sitting, and crying. People walked past me as though I wasn't even there. I felt like a ghost.

Emotional abuse changes the structure of a child's brain. Repeated messages of derision and scorn result in deeply entrenched neural pathways, internalized and ultimately adopted by the child *as their own voice*. Over time this self-loathing response attaches to more and more thoughts, feelings, and behaviors. Eventually, any inclination toward authentic self-expression activates these internal networks of self-loathing. Our inner world is often in a state of self-attack. The ability to defend, support, or nurture ourselves is severely inhibited. Over time, our neural pathways expand into a large complex network that dominates mental activity, driving profound anxiety, and invoking shame just as it did in our past.

Until these messages are deconstructed, a survivor may live in varying degrees of emotional flashback much of the time. Somatically and emotionally, the past continues to live. The world remains a frightening place long after the actual threats are gone. A childhood rife with verbal and emotional abuse can make an inner critic voice feel like the *truth*, like our actual *identity*. Over time, binge eating becomes a way to soothe or distract from this ongoing internal attack.

▶ COPING BY HIDING: FRAGMENTING OUR VOICES

When complex trauma is involved, a child does not have adequate time or support to regain emotional equilibrium between occurrences of damaging events. They are often left with the knowledge that it can happen again at any time, leading to states of ongoing vigilance, anticipation, and anxiety. Rather than having a secure and relatively safe childhood, children become worried and hyper-vigilant. *The psychological energy that would normally go to learning, exploration, and development instead goes to coping and survival.* It is this fundamental loss of self-development that leaves enormous holes in the ability to self-soothe, problem solve, and call on support systems in times of distress. It becomes necessary, from this world of danger, to go it alone, hide any signs of vulnerability, and avoid being seen.

> I will go over and over interactions with my friends. Did my boss think something I did was stupid? Is my friend mad at me for being late?
> I almost never have an interaction that just feels fine and that I don't rethink over and over.

> I can remember embarrassing moments with incredible clarity. I'll replay them over and over.

> No one really knows me. Some people know some things, but I'm not
> all of me anywhere. Something is always tucked away.

Hypersensitivity to others' moods is common too. Survivors may be more aware of others' feelings and needs than their own.

> I know exactly how my Dad is feeling when he walks in the room.
> I know the kind of night it's going to be immediately. I had no idea
> how angry I was about having to pay this much attention to my Dad's
> drinking and his mood. I didn't even know it was reasonable to have
> feelings about it at all.

Many people with histories of complex trauma also feel a sense of being "on" or feeling like an "actor" in their own lives.

> I don't really feel close to people. They think I'm connecting with them,
> but inside, I have erected a big wall between us.

> I am a slightly different person with everyone, and myself with no one.
> My default setting is chameleon.

> I hate when people from different parts of my life come together. I feel
> like I have to be a hundred different people at once.

As a result of this acting, social isolation can be a significant problem for people with BED. Since being in relationships can feel like a tremendous amount of work, people often feel a constant struggle between wanting to connect and wanting to disconnect.

> The anticipation of what might go wrong is overwhelming. It is so hard
> just to leave the house. I fight with myself for hours or even days about
> going to social events. Going to see friends or going out at all, even
> though I know I'll feel better if I do, feels like so much effort.

When people decide not to go out, they often feel, in addition to the isolation, shame and anger toward themselves. They are at a very high risk for binge eating as a result.

> When I decide not to go somewhere, I feel relief first and foremost.
> I don't have to do the dance of self-presentation. And it always turns

into a binge. It's partly shame at failing to do what I know is best, partly to stave off loneliness and sadness about missing out, and partly because I feel so angry and exhausted from the struggle.

People with relationship trauma in their histories also tend to have difficulties communicating needs to others and keeping self-protective boundaries. Many people with such histories tend to allow unsafe others to remain in their lives, reinforcing the story that safe intimacy is impossible.

Sexual relationships may be especially difficult, resulting in further loneliness and isolation. This is particularly true when the person has been a victim of sexual or physical violence. Poor body image can be compounded by such circumstances. Many with BED believe their bodies could not possibly be attractive to a sexual partner, and this narrative is strongly culturally sanctioned. There can even be a certain kind of protection in such body shame.

Hating my body is protective because I keep to myself. I stay home. I stay invisible. I don't draw attention. I have issues around sex and sexuality and I've avoided relationships, in part because of my eating and body issues. I don't put myself out there because I'm fat. I don't have to take risks. I don't have to be proven wrong if I don't try. I tell myself no one wants me or my body and it's easier to believe that when I don't have evidence to the contrary. It's not logical because a lack of proof shouldn't be proof, but somehow it feels true.

Being "sexy" with someone has always felt like an act. It has never had anything to do with me. I'm doing what is expected until I can get it over with.

▶ MY FAULT

People with significant relationship traumas believe they somehow *deserved* what happened to them. Especially in the mind of a child, this conclusion of personal responsibility for bad things happening provides an explanation for something inexplicable, and lets critical caregivers off the hook of blame. Indeed, we are neurologically and developmentally compelled to come to this conclusion; it keeps us working to adapt to the family system and thus have some measure of care and protection. But what works to keep the family system going is not always good for the person's development and well-being long-term.

> Years of criticism and condemnation from my father took a toll. I am the burden he convinced me I was. I am the insensitive, unappreciative, selfish, demanding obligation he told me I was. Or so the voice in my head continues to cry, shout, slice, and tear into me. The scars are deep. The wounds never fully healed. My picking at the scabs keeps them raw and fresh.

As a result of this kind internalization of shaming messages, trauma survivors often feel marked for struggle and failure. There is an acceptance of blame and a conditioned self-loathing.

> No matter what I do, say, or accomplish, I always know I was bad enough for my mom to leave our family. That will always be what happened, and I fear I will always think I drove her away. I landed in foster care because I was just not good enough.

This begs some very existential questions as we develop. What is the point of this entire struggle? Hopelessness and depression make sense from such a vantage point.

> I never fit in. I never felt right. Something was *always* off. And it seems to *always* be me. Round peg in a square hole. Trying so hard to change, to shift, to adapt, fit in. And never succeeding. I'm exhausted. Food is my refuge.

If childhood was unsafe physically or emotionally in these ways, the world can feel like a dangerous, judgmental place. It can feel difficult to trust others, or believe we have a right to get needs met or be treated with respect. When this is the case, we tend to have something called a negativity bias. We seek out and identify possible threats and dangers. This can be an adaptive strategy when there are real threats. Over time, however this negativity bias keeps us on a state of yellow alert, even when any actual threat has long passed. Such ongoing activation may play a powerful role in needing to find a mechanism like binge eating to soothe.

> My dad often would warn me about predators and kidnappers. How strangers could snatch me up in the blink of an eye, how the world wasn't safe, and that I wasn't capable. He dismissed that I was in karate, that I would scream for help, that I would be careful, that I wasn't riding my bike that far. It didn't matter. I clearly didn't know what I was talking about. I wasn't safe. It was only a matter of time before some big burly guy would grab me and take off with me. What does this have to do with eating? Well, it's connected because it's about my body. It's about not feeling confident or secure. It's about safety. It's about the likelihood that I'll be violated. I have no power. I'm just always waiting for a man to take advantage of me. How, then, do I know how to be around men? How am I supposed to be attractive, but not also feel in danger?

> The feeling is an anticipation that something very bad, even irreversible is about to happen if I don't do my part right. I get flooded and confused by fear. There are no perceived gradations. Everything is scaled at 100%.

> I never believe things will work out. I figure it's safest if I assume chaos and loss. That way, things won't broadside me, like they did in the past.

> Anxious, restless, bored, lonely. Fear. Avoidance. Shame. Feeling less than. Feeling young, small, stupid. Messy house. Feeling overwhelmed. Too much to do, never get it all done. Not good enough. Never going to get it all done, never going to get better, never going to lose weight, never going to be in a relationship. Hopelessness. Panic, frantic, anxiety. This [voice] hits at my deep, deep lack of safety. I didn't get a sense of security, a sense of "I'm okay" growing up and I still have that. It's a deep-seated heavily entrenched fear. I'm constantly afraid. Of everything.

Due to such fears about safety and acceptance, many with BED describe a sense of acting in their lives, of rarely being themselves even in the most mundane situations.

> I'm not even real in the drug store. I'm standing in line, worrying about what people are thinking about me, my weight, and what I'm buying.

> I'm thinking about how my stomach sticks out in line at the damn drug store with people I don't even know!

Even those who would describe themselves as outgoing or extroverted are working to present themselves to others.

> I'm only me at home. Otherwise, I'm on stage. I know what is expected, and that's what I do. What I *want* doesn't even enter into the equation.

> I am always afraid people will see how crazy I am underneath. I'm just sure that my real feelings must be wrong.

> I always look the part of the executive. Perfectly put together, right answers, and work done. But this is not how I want to dress, or think or be. I want to work in a bookstore and wear sweatpants. No wonder I wear them, and read, when I binge.

> I'm not an agent of change in my own life. Life is about others' approval and I have to do that which is expected.

Many of my clients with BED describe their lives in terms that are about performance and success. Choices, in their minds, should not be based on needs or desires. They should be made based on what they consider responsible; that which their families and cultures expect them to do. Bingeing is the one way to be out of control.

▶ IMPACT ON A DEVELOPING MIND

When children feel safe and attachments in their lives are mostly reliable and healthy, the brain follows a known developmental path. Research by Schore (2003), Siegel and Solomon (2003), Badenoch (2017), and others tells us early relationships shape the area of the brain known as the prefrontal cortex. This is the part of the brain that helps a child regulate their nervous system and manage emotions. It also helps quell the response of the amygdala, a tiny part of the brain responsible for detecting fear, preparing for emergency responses, and processing reward and emotions. A healthy prefrontal cortex serves to integrate our ability to attune well to ourselves and others, and to have empathy and compassion. It is the part of the brain that allows us to be aware of our own internal experience (sometimes clinically referred to as our "observing ego"). In short, this part of the brain allows for resiliency in times of stress. It allows us to notice and effectively interpret feelings and experiences without being swept away by them. It is our best buffer against being overwhelmed by fear and shame, and the best protection from development of coping mechanisms like binge eating. If early important attachments to others have been inadequate or sufficiently damaging, the full development of the prefrontal cortex is derailed. Critical strategies for self-care, compassion, and resiliency in the face of danger and loss, are compromised.

When yearnings for connection are met often enough with positive responses, they are paired in our neural circuitry; this coupling becomes the internal working model of how we expect relationships to be. When connection is available, we feel secure, safe, loved, and lovable. If, on the other hand, such yearning is met often enough with responses that harm us physically or give the sense that we are unlovable, our brain structure develops in such a way as to anticipate other relationships will hurt us in the same way. In other words, we learn from experience. This is not pathology; it is survival. The younger we learn something is intrinsic to survival, the better we learn the lesson. Due to the recursive nature of shame, our neural connections become pathogenic and block learning. *Even with accomplishments, even with love, even with evidence to the contrary, these implicit neural nets remain dissociated from the integrating flow of the brain, locking the person into the original shaming events.* It is for this reason that changing our shaming narratives is so difficult. Even though we are able to see others with compassion and gentleness, when it comes to assessing our own worth and value, our earliest stories filled with fear and shame are the strongest. It is for this reason that we cannot simply "get over it." We are hardwired to maintain these formative narratives, experiencing them not as *beliefs*, but as *truth*. They do not feel false, even when we rationally know them to be. As a result of this neurological adaptation to an unsafe world, symptoms such as binge eating develop over time to soothe the frequent experience of inadequacy.

For many with BED, weight loss becomes a seductive way to change the shame narrative—to gain social acceptance, feel others' approval, and be heard and seen. Obsessive dieting and weight loss efforts, all strongly socially sanctioned, can serve as distraction from our unmet desires for intimacy, connection, joy, and peace. There is something we can do, so we believe, to finally fix our broken places.

▶ SHAMING OF MANY KINDS

In addition to damage suffered at the hands of caregivers or other important adults, discrimination and stigma throughout our lives based on weight, gender, race, culture, socioeconomic class, religion, sexual orientation, gender identity, health status, and physical ability can also be traumatizing, teaching people to feel shame about who they are or the bodies in which they live. When these factors co-occur, the impact is compounded. This is called intersectionality, and it heightens the risk of, among many things, developing BED. Food can be a coping mechanism to psychologically check out from these profound and widespread forms of shaming. Binge eating can allow some sense of power by breaking rules, a way to vent anger by directing it at one's body, and to both release and inflict pain.

For those who find themselves at the intersection of marginalized social groups, shame narratives from both present and past combine, reinforcing the impact. According to Gloria Lucas, a Latina leader and founder of Nalgona Positivity Pride (Sutriasa, 2017) "Many of us have bruised family lineages from historical atrocities such as slavery, genocide and colonization. We were often given unhealthy messages around food, body autonomy, and self-love. On top of that, we have to live through current systemic racism, modern colonialism, sexism, heteropatriarchy and sizeism." Historical atrocities that have traumatized people of color and indigenous people are not simply erased by the passage of time—they leave future generations in psychological and cultural distress, and commonly economic distress as well. This is called the transgeneration of trauma.

> I was always told that I had to be extra careful being black. Don't talk back if you're alone, don't make a fuss if you're stopped by police. My generation fights back a lot more, but that fear is always there.

> Stories of the Holocaust were part of the fabric of the family. My grandmother survived as a little girl, and I knew it could always happen again. I was not supposed to do anything that could be judged, or that might stand out. In addition, being fat was seen as being selfish. If

there might again be a scarcity of food, I was assumed to have taken more than my share.

Because eating disorders have been diagnosed so often for white, straight, young, wealthy, thin women, the experiences of binge eating disorder for indigenous people and people of color is largely unknown, likely underreported and underdiagnosed. Binge eating can serve a powerful function if daily experience is chaotic and dangerous. If our body feels targeted and shamed, and if we live in fear of violence and oppression, an eating disorder makes sense. "Worrying about scarcity is our culture's version of post-traumatic stress. It happens when we've been through too much, and rather than coming together to heal (which requires vulnerability) we're angry and scared and at each other's throats" (Brown, 2012).

▶ LOSS OF THE REAL TRUTH

Tara Brach (2001) refers to the mindset created by frequent shame messages as the "trance of unworthiness." Beliefs and feelings of deficiency prevent intimacy and authenticity with anyone—we sense we are intrinsically flawed and others will find out. Because the fear of failure is so powerful and consistent, it is difficult to lay down the tools of hyper-vigilance and believe we will be safe. We become consumed with hiding flaws and thus are not living the moment-to-moment experience of our lives. Brach (2001) describes the impact of this trance: "This experience of personal deficiency is a pervasive form of suffering, with its roots in societal norms that assign superior value to certain races, types of intelligence, appearance, sexual orientation, behavior, and performance. Basically, the familiar message is, "Your natural way of being is not okay; to be acceptable you must be different from the way you are." As a colleague put it, "Our innocent childhood dance (of acceptability) is slammed in mid-pirouette." The desire to reach out and engage immediately contracts—we withdraw, shut down, hide. Our hearts break.

> I cannot do anything without second guessing myself, without feeling scared someone will be angry with me. This takes up so much of my life. I am constantly afraid I will be exposed for being bad. I focus on believing there is something wrong with me. And what is wrong with me is being fat.

One client told me the story of putting a soda can in her mother's purse for safekeeping when she was a little girl. The movement and heat over the course of a day at the fair made the can explode, leaking soda everywhere. Her mother screamed at her, accused her of being stupid, short-sighted, and inconsiderate. She was slapped publicly. The shame was overwhelming; there was no option but to believe she should somehow have known about the chemistry of the unopened soda. Another client recalls her father losing any interest in her when she reached puberty. He wanted a controllable little doll, not an empowered young woman. By simply getting older, she believed she had somehow done something egregious. As a result, to be safe, we make our lives increasingly small, isolated, and confined. Our dreams, passions, and desires shut down and go unexpressed. Creativity suffers. The things that make us unique are cast aside, buried, hidden.

▶ IMPLEMENTING THE FIRST PRACTICE: MEETING AND ACCEPTING OUR PARTS

The first practice, honoring the impact of history, is the step upon which the remaining build. It is the best way to build compassion and gentleness for the process of healing from BED. It allows you to fully understand and appreciate how and why binge eating has developed in your life, and the forces that sustain it now.

To truly honor the impact of history, we need to recognize how our experiences, both past and present, cultural and individual, have impacted the way we respond to the world around us. It is critical to remember that making this change will not feel normal, comfortable, or even acceptable. As we will discuss in the coming pages, even change we know is for the best will probably feel threatening to long-held notions of what keeps us safe. This will change over time; it will be increasingly safe to be as good to yourself as you probably are to those you love most.

For the first practice of honoring the past, consider the following.

- ▶ It is OK to talk with trusted others about your history. Saying the truth heals.

- ▶ Try to gently challenge the shame game about having BED; you binge for good reasons, not for lack of willpower.

▶ Resistance to change is about fear and self-protection. It is *not* about a desire to stay stuck or not wanting change badly enough.

▶ Change feels wrong and uncomfortable for quite a while. It does integrate into a new reality over time, and with practice.

▶ Anxiety and depression, like BED itself, can be responses to things you believe you cannot change, survive, or escape. They are not signs of weakness, but the way we are wired to cope with inescapable, damaging experiences.

▶ Weight, socioeconomic class, race, gender, gender identity, sexual orientation, and physical ability play roles in shame narratives. Your inner shame voice is not simply distorted cognition, but incorporates *real cultural messages around you.*

▶ In our culture, the definition of success includes being incredibly busy, frantic and always striving for the next win; recovery asks you to consider a different balance.

▶ Give yourself permission to feel things you do not expect and cannot explain.

▶ Give yourself time to heal; don't judge the pace of your recovery.

▶ Expect to be tired and to need extra tending in this work.

▶ Expect and envision a life without (or with less) binge eating, even if it seems impossible right now.

▶ Try to remember the presence of fear does *not* have to mean there is real danger.

▶ Feelings are real and acceptable; they are not always *accurate.*

▶ Shaming your feelings makes them much harder to move through; feelings pass, but self-recrimination sticks

▶ Know that pain will pass.

▶ You will be safe and loved; there is love out there for you.

▶ You will find your people.

▶ You are not alone on this journey.

▶ Remember, you do not need to explain or defend your experience, even if it differs from others.

▶ Your body is your home. It has been waiting for you to return and care for it, probably for a long time. You can learn to trust its wisdom.

▶ You would not be here if you were not strong, compassionate, and capable of keeping yourself safe.

In the next chapter, you will learn how to meet the urges to binge, and the best ways to begin planting the seeds for stepping into your authentic life and body. For the moment, before you turn the page, try and simply honor all you have done to survive.

▶ BIBLIOGRAPHY

Andreyeva, T., Puhl, R. M., & Brownell, K. D. (2008). Changes in perceived weight discrimination among Americans, 1995–1996 through 2004–2006. *Obesity (Silver Spring)*, *16*(5), 1129–1134. Retrieved from http://doi.org/10.1038/oby.2008.35.

Annis, N. M., Cash, T. F., & Hrabosky, J. I. (2004). Body image and psychosocial differences among stable average weight, currently overweight, and formerly overweight women: The role of stigmatizing experiences. *Journal of Body Image*, *1*(2), 155–167. Retrieved from http://doi.org/10.1016/j.bodyim.2003.12.001.

Ashmore, J. A., Friedman, K. E., Reichmann, S. K., & Musante, G. (2008). Weight-based stigmatization, psychological distress, and binge eating behavior among obese treatment-seeking adults. *Journal of Eating Behavior*, *9*(2), 203–209. Retrieved from http://doi.org/10.1016/j.eatbeh.2007.09.006.

Badenoch, B. (2017). *The heart of trauma: Healing the embodied brain in the context of relationships*. New York, NY: W. W. Norton & Company, Inc.

Bauer, K. W., Yang, Y. W., & Austin, S. B. (2004, February). "How can we stay healthy when you're throwing all of this in front of us?" Findings from focus groups and interviews in middle schools on environmental influences on nutrition and physical activity. *Health Education and Behavior, 31*(1), 34–46. Retrieved from http://doi.org/10.1177/1090198103255372.

Becker, D. F., & Grilo, C. M. (2011). Childhood maltreatment in women with binge-eating disorder: Associations with psychiatric comorbidity, psychological functioning, and eating pathology. *Eating and Weight Disorders, 16*(2), e113–e120.

Bishop, E. (2010). *Innate temperament and eating disorder treatment.* Retrieved from www.addictionpro.com/article/innate-temperament-and-eating-disorder-treatment.

Brach, T. (2001). Awakening from the trance of unworthiness. *Inquiring Mind, 17*(2). Retrieved from www.tarabrach.com/articles-interviews/inquiring-trance/.

Brewerton, T. D. (2007). Eating disorders, trauma, and comorbidity: Focus on PTSD. *The Journal of Treatment & Prevention, 15*(4), 285–304. Retrieved from http://doi.org/10.1080/10640260701454311.

Brown, B. (2012). *Daring greatly: How the courage to be vulnerable transforms the way we live, love, parent, and lead.* New York, NY: Avery.

Browne, A. (1993). Violence against women by male partners: Prevention, outcomes and policy implications. *American Psychologist, 48*, 1077–1087.

Browne, A., & Finkelhor, D. (1986). Impact of child sexual abuse: A review of the research. *Psychology Bulletin, 99*, 66–77. Retrieved from http://doi.org/10.1037/0033-2909.99.1.66.

Courtois, C. (2010). *Understanding complex trauma, complex reactions, and treatment approaches.* Retrieved from www.giftfromwithin.org/html/cptsd-understanding-treatment.html.

Dunkley, D. M., Masheb, R. M., & Grilo, C. M. (2010). Childhood maltreatment, depressive symptoms, and body dissatisfaction in patients with binge eating disorder: The mediating role of self-criticism. *International Journal of Eating Disorders, 43*, 274–281.

Fisher, J. (2017). *Healing the fragmented selves of trauma survivors: Overcoming internal self-alienation.* New York, NY: Routledge.

Friedman, K. E., Ashmore, J. A., & Applegate, K. L. (2008, November 16). Recent experiences of weight-based stigmatization in a weight loss surgery population: Psychological and behavioral correlates. *Obesity (Silver Spring)*, Supplement 2, S69–S74. Retrieved from http://doi.org/10.1038/oby.2008.457.

Friedman, K. E., Reichmann, S. K., Costanzo, P. R., Zelli, A., Ashmore, J. A., & Musante, G. J. (2005). Weight stigmatization and ideological beliefs: Relation to psychological functioning in obese adults. *Obesity Research, 13*(5), 907–916. Retrieved from http://doi.org/10.1038/oby.2005.105.

Goldberg, J., True, W. R., Eisen, S. A., & Henderson, H. (1990). A twin study of the effects of the Vietnam War on posttraumatic stress disorder. *Journal of the American Medical Association, 263*, 1227–1232. Retrieved from www.ncbi.nlm.nih.gov/pubmed/2304238.

Grilo, C. M., & Masheb, R. M. (2001). Childhood psychological, physical, and sexual maltreatment in outpatients with binge eating disorder: Frequency and associations with gender, obesity, and eating-related psychopathology. *Obesity Research, 9*(5), 320–325. Retrieved from http://doi.org/10.1038/oby.2001.40.

Haines, J., Neumark-Sztainer, D., Eisenberg, M. E., & Hannan, P. J. (2006). Weight teasing and disordered eating behaviors in adolescents: Longitudinal findings from Project EAT (Eating Among Teens). *Pediatrics, 117*(2), e209–e215. Retrieved from http://doi.org/10.1542/peds.2005-1242.

Hatzenbuehler, M. L., Keyes, K. M., & Hasin, D. S. (2009). Associations between perceived weight discrimination and the prevalence of psychiatric disorders in the general population. *Obesity (Silver Spring), 17*(11), 2033–2039. Retrieved from http://doi.org/10.1038/oby.2009.131.

Herman, J. (1992). *Trauma and recovery.* New York, NY: Basic Books.

Herman, J. L. (1992). Complex PTSD: A syndrome in survivors of prolonged and repeated trauma. *Journal of Traumatic Stress, 5*(3), 377–391. Retrieved from http://dx.doi.org/10.1002/jts.2490050305.

Herrin, M., & Matsumoto, N. (2011, March). The truth about so-called sugar addiction. In E. Triboli & E. Resch (Eds.), *Eating disorder news.* IntuitiveEating.org as retrieved from www.intuitiveeating.org/category/binge-eating/.

Jackson, T. D., Grilo, C. M., & Masheb, R. M. (2000). Teasing history, onset of obesity, current eating disorder psychopathology, body dissatisfaction, and psychological functioning in binge eating disorder. *Obesity Research, 8*(6). Retrieved from http://doi.org/451-8.10.1038/oby.2000.56.

Kendall-Tackett, K. A., Williams, L. M., & Finkelhor, D. (1993). Impact of sexual abuse on children: A review and synthesis. *Psychological Bulletin, 113*, 164–180. Retrieved from www.ncbi.nlm.nih.gov/pubmed/8426874.

Linehan, M. (2015). *DBT skills training manual.* New York, NY: The Guilford Press.

Malinosky-Rummell, R., & Hansen, D. J. (1993). Long term consequences of child-hood physical abuse. *Psychological Bulletin, 144*, 68–79. Retrieved from http://dx.doi.org/10.1037/0033-2909.114.1.68.

Michopoulos, V., Powers, A., Moore, C., Villarreal, S., Ressler, K. J., & Bradley, B. (2015). The mediating role of emotion dysregulation and depression on the rela-tionship between childhood trauma exposure and emotional eating. *Appetite, 91*, 129–136. Retrieved from http://doi.org/10.1016/j.eppet.2015.03.036.

Mitchell, K. S., Mazzeo, S. E., Schlesinger, M. R., Brewerton, T. D., & Smith, B. N. (2012). Comorbidity of partial and subthreshold PTSD among men and women with eating disorders in the National Comorbidity Survey Replication study. *International Journal of Eating Disorders, 45*(3), 285–304. Retrieved from http://doi.org/10.1080/10640260701454311.

Myers, A., & Rosen, J. C. (1999). Obesity stigmatization and coping: Relation to mental health symptoms, body image, and self-esteem. *International Journal of Obesity, 23*(3), 221–230. Retrieved from www.ncbi.nlm.nih.gov/pubmed/10193866.

National Center for Health Statistics. (2006). *Prevalence of overweight and obesity among adults: United States, 2003–2004.* Retrieved from www.cdc.gov/nchs/data/hestat/overweight/overweight_adult_03.htm.

Ogden, P., & Fisher, J. (2015). *Sensorimotor psychotherapy: Interventions for trauma and attachment.* New York, NY: W. W. Norton & Company, Inc.

Palmisano, G. L., Innamorati, M., & Vanderlinden, J. (2016). Life adverse experi-ences in relation with obesity and binge eating disorder: A systematic review. *Journal of Behavioral Addiction, 5*(1), 11–31. Retrieved from http://doi.org/10.1556/2006.5.2016.018.

Pingitore, R., Dugoni, B. L., Tindale, R. S., & Spring, B. (1994). Bias against over-weight job applicants in a simulated employment interview. *Journal of Applied Psychology, 79*(6), 909–917. Retrieved from http://citeseerx.ist.psu.edu/viewdoc/download?doi=10.1.1.468.3727&rep=rep1&type=pdf.

Porges, S. W. (2017). *The pocket guide to the polyvagal theory: The transformative power of feeling safe* (Norton series on interpersonal neurobiology). New York, NY: W. W. Norton & Company, Inc.

Puhl, R. M., & Brownell, K. D. (2006). Confronting and coping with weight stigma: An investigation of overweight and obese adults. *Obesity (Silver Spring), 14*(10), 1802–1815.

Puhl, R. M., & Heuer, C. A. (2010). Obesity stigma: Important considerations for public health. *American Journal of Public Health, 100*(6), 1019–1028. Retrieved from http://doi.org/10.2105/AJPH2009.159491.

Puhl, R. M., & King, K. M. (2013). Weight discrimination and bullying. *Best Practice & Research Clinical Endocrinology & Metabolism, 27*(2), 117–127. Retrieved from http://doi.org/10.1016/j.beem.2012./12/002.

Puhl, R. M., Moss-Racusin, C. A., & Schwartz, M. B. (2007). Internalization of weight bias: Implications for binge eating and emotional well-being. *Obesity (Silver Spring), 15*(1), 19–23. Retrieved from http://doi.org/10.1038/oby.2007.521.

Putnam, F. W. (1997). *Dissociation in children and adolescents.* New York, NY: The Guilford Press.

Rosenberger, P. H., Henderson, K. E., & Grilo, C. M. (2006). Correlates of body image dissatisfaction in extremely obese female bariatric surgery candidates. *Obesity Surgery, 16*(10), 1331–1336.

Roth, S., Newman, E., Pelcovitz, D., van der Kolk, B. A., & Mandel, F. S. (1997). Complex PTSD in victims exposed to sexual and physical abuse: Results from the DSM-IV field trial for posttraumatic stress disorder. *Journal of Traumatic Stress, 10,* 539–555. Retrieved from www.ncbi.nlm.nih.gov/pubmed/9391940.

Russell, D. E. H. (1986). *The secret trauma: Incest in the lives of girls and women.* New York, NY: Basic Books.

Schore, A. N. (2003, May 17). *Affect regulation and the origin of the self.* New York: W. W. Norton & Company.

Siegel, D. (2001). *The developing mind: How relationships and the brain interact to shape who we are.* New York, NY: The Guilford Press.

Siegel, D. (2010). *The mindful therapist: A clinician's guide to mindsight and neural integration* (Norton series on interpersonal neurobiology). New York, NY: W. W. Norton & Company, Inc.

Siegel, D. (2010). *Mindsight: The new science of personal transformation.* New York, NY: Bantam.

Siegel, D. J., & Hartzell, M. (2013). *Parenting from the inside out: How a deeper self-understanding can help you raise children who thrive.* New York, NY: TarcherPerigee.

Siegel, D., & Solomon, M. (2003). *Healing trauma: Attachment, mind, body and brain* (Norton series on interpersonal neurobiology). New York, NY: W. W. Norton & Company, Inc.

Stevelos, J. (2014). Bullying, bullycide and childhood obesity. *Obesity Action Coalition.* Retrieved from www.obesityaction.org/educational-resources/

resource-articles-2/childhood-obesity-resource-articles/bullying-bullycide-and-childhood-obesity.

Sutriasa, A. (2017, December 17). How to decolonize the way you think about your body. *Yes! Magazine.* Retrieved from www.yesmagazine.org/peace-justice/how-to-decolonize-the-way-you-think-about-your-body-20171214.

Sweezy, M., & Ziskind, E. L. (Eds.). (2013). *Internal family systems therapy: New dimensions.* New York, NY: Routledge.

Terr, L. (1991). Childhood traumas: An outline and overview. *American Journal of Psychiatry, 148*(1), 10–20. Retrieved from http://doi.org/10.1176/ajp.148.1.10.

van der Kolk, B. A. (1991). The compulsion to repeat the trauma: Re-enactment, revictimization, and masochism. *Psychiatric Clinics of North America, 12,* 389–411. Retrieved from www.ncbi.nlm.nih.gov/pubmed/2664732.

van der Kolk, B. A. (2005). Developmental trauma disorder. *Psychiatric Annals, 35*(5), 401–406.

van der Kolk, B. A., Perry, J. C., & Herman, J. L. (1991). Childhood origins of self-destructive behavior. *American Journal of Psychiatry, 148,* 1665–1671. Retrieved from http://doi.org/10.1176/ajp.148.12.1665.

Walker, P. (2013). *Complex PTSD from surviving to thriving: A guide and map for recovering from childhood trauma.* Charleston, SC: CreateSpace Independent Publishing Platform.

3

Taking Your POWR Back

My world turned upside down in my early teens and set the stage for my eating disorder to fully blossom. It kept me functioning at a time when I wanted to disappear. It allowed me to cope when there seemed to be no other way. It was my escape when life was too real. It was my companion when I was alone.

I was 14 when my mother's alcoholism escalated, the family business failed, we lost our home, my parents separated, and I was forced to begin ninth grade in a new school.

"Good night Chev," my father said as he kissed me on the forehead that Christmas evening. It was the holiday before my parents filed for divorce and he spent the day with my mother, brother, and me in our little apartment. He lived elsewhere with a friend, but we had no idea of the location or how to reach him except during the day at his work number. We did not see him often and this day together made me yearn for what I had lost.

"When will I see you again?" I asked.

"I'll give you a call and we can get together for dinner some day after work." He left my room and walked down the hallway toward the front door. I recall the long, slow creak of the door opening and closing. He turned the key in the deadbolt and the screen door slammed closed behind him. I listened to the scrape of his shoes on the pavement as he walked to his car. As he drove away, I hung on to the sound of the engine revving and gears shifting until his car was no longer discernible amid the general hum of traffic. I began to sob.

Despite a good day together as a family, I knew the changes to my family were permanent. I put all hope of being whole again aside for the final time. I knew when my father left that evening, I was on my own. No longer could I trust the adults in my life to take my needs into consideration.

Mom spent her days working menial jobs and trying to deal with her new reality as a divorcée. She drank a lot and I worried she would die as a result. She would disappear at times, and I would often find myself awake at 3 a.m. watching out the window for her car.

Binges became a daily requirement to lessen my anxiety. They came at a price: increased self-hate and loathing my body. I felt so alone and unloved. I wondered who would want to be around a binge eating, fat, disgusting, ugly teenager. The next few years were full of risk-taking, rebellion, and a nod to my every whim and impulse.

Money and food were scarce, so it became necessary for me to plan my binges around opportunities to find money or food. I stole both from family and friends whenever the opportunity arose. During one incredibly difficult evening, I broke in to our neighbor's apartment when I discovered they were not home. I knew they kept their sliding glass door unlocked and with heart pounding, I quickly raided their refrigerator and pantry. I stuffed the bologna, processed cheese, white bread, instant mashed potatoes, milk and butter into a paper bag and ran home quickly.

The time spent eating my stash that evening was memorable because of the effort required. I barely tasted the food and could not feel my body or feelings. I escaped into the TV and the chaos around me disappeared. I ate several more sandwiches and washed each one down with a giant bowl of the vanilla ice cream my grandmother had brought us when she visited the previous day. By the time the binge ended, I was so full I had trouble breathing and could think of nothing except how much I hated myself. I vowed, as I did with every binge, that the following day would be different. I would eat as little as possible and chart a plan to lose weight. I went to bed and slept, waking only occasionally, for two days.

Throughout my teen years, I added alcohol, drugs, and dysfunctional and/or abusive relationships to my a la carte menu of dissociative substances and behaviors. I attempted college twice after high school before giving up and moving to Washington, D.C., to work dead end jobs, party in nightclubs, and engage in all the risky behaviors that would keep me numb and disconnected. I had no sense of accountability to myself or others. I lived paycheck to paycheck, and never thought further into the future than my next binge, diet, drink, or night out on the town.

Drinking, drugging, and partying quickly accelerated and put me in questionable situations around questionable people. During the final chapter of this part of my life, I drove around dangerous neighborhoods looking for crack cocaine, was shot at, and became homeless. After a week of sleeping on friends' couches and in seedy motels, I finally called my brother and asked him to pick me up to take me to my grandparents' home where I could live and figure out what to do next.

I was at the end of a long descent from any of the promise my life once held. My health had been ravaged by the cycles of bingeing and restricting, overconsumption of alcohol and cigarettes, stress, lack of sleep, and the general anxiety that goes along with a life of uncertainty and victimization at the hands of those who take advantage of the vulnerable. I knew that if I did not get help I was going to die by my own hands or as a result of the harm I was doing to my body.

▶ BED AND A FRAGMENTED INNER WORLD

You become. It takes a long time. That's why it doesn't happen often to people who break easily, or have sharp edges, or who have to be carefully kept. Generally, by the time you are Real, most of your hair has been loved off, and your eyes drop out and you get loose in your joints and very shabby. But these things don't matter at all, because once you are Real you can't be ugly, except to people who don't understand.

—Margery Williams on the wisdom of the Velveteen Rabbit

I remember my first therapist asked me how aware I was of my own inner world. What emotions did I feel? What thoughts did I have? How was my body reacting to the world? When did I feel most safe? Most vulnerable? I had only the vaguest idea what she was talking about. Listening to my needs, much less meeting them, was a foreign idea. I knew what was going on inside my heart and mind only insofar as I kept track of all the ways I might disappoint someone or how someone had disappointed me. I had considerable awareness of what I had done wrong, or would no doubt do wrong soon. I was always on "yellow alert," anticipating the next shameful experience, particularly about my body. How would I avoid going to the beach this weekend so I wouldn't have to wear a swimsuit? Would I be able to lose weight by the graduation/wedding/vacation? Would I resist the temptation to binge today? My critic voice harped constantly, assessing missteps and figuring out how to best present myself to others. And that critique was not limited to my body, of course. Was my friend angry with me for being late last week? Did I talk too much at the party? Did I look stupid in front of my colleagues? At some point, I would feel anger and rebellion in response to this shame and fear, and my "screw it" voice that so often accompanied a binge would rear her head. Afterward, my critic part returned with even greater vitriol, and the cycle started again. Ultimately, I had competing parts inside, all saying different things, but each ultimately trying to be safe. I felt alienated, out of the flow of life itself, never able to relax or let my guard down in the presence of others. This simply felt like the nature of reality itself. I had no idea the world didn't have to feel this way.

Strangely though, in other parts of my adult life, I felt confident, capable, and basically "OK." I managed my responsibilities, and I made fairly sound financial decisions. I had close friends who cared about me, and who I cared about, and a husband I loved. Why couldn't I always feel access to this capable part of me? Why could I not direct this strong, kind, protective voice toward myself? This aspect of me felt like a healthy adult, one who didn't even want to binge; in fact, it didn't seem to have an eating disorder at all. It felt like "the real me." Yet somehow, this energy seemed to disappear when I was going for the food. It was as though something else took over my brain. I felt absolutely hijacked by a force I couldn't stop. I wondered if I might be crazy. Turns out, many people with BED feel this way. And there are very good reasons for it.

When we are young, safety is the most powerful driving force for all of us. With the right care, we can survive profound hardships, including physical and psychological threat and harm, many kinds of pain, and major losses. When we face physical or psychological threats to our safety, especially as children, we instinctively prioritize connection to our caregivers (called our attachment drive) above all else, even beyond our flight/fight mechanism (fighting and fleeing are not good survival options for children; it is not until adolescence that we begin to enact these ways of dealing with threat).

We adapt to the rules laid down, whether reasonable and protective, or damaging and chaotic. While such adaptation allows us to socialize and survive, we pay a high price if the rules force us to segregate and disconnect from aspects of our emotional, somatic, and depending on age, cognitive, experience of the world. Using a skill at which the human brain excels, we compartmentalize our internal world, losing conscious access to the truth about who we are, what we feel, and what we need. We maintain this disconnection well after danger has passed; the remaining fragments lurk outside our awareness, triggering intense shame when they do appear. Binge eating is one effective way to maintain the divide, keeping us numb to our experience, and detached from ourselves and others.

> My mother got violent when she drank. She would slap us for no reason at all, somehow just enraged by our presence. I was terrified she was going to leave us alone, that she was sick of us. When she sobered up, it was like nothing ever happened. It was never mentioned. So, I just shut away the terrified part of me and played along, thankful that it was over. I feel that fear now when my husband gets angry. He would never hit me, but I feel small and terrified all the same. The terror just comes out of nowhere and takes me over. He isn't my husband in that moment, he's my mother.
>
> I felt so much shame at being from the wrong neighborhood at my school. Whenever I am around people in the "in crowd," I'm trying so hard to be one of them. I'll sell my soul, who I really am, just to be included. I pride myself normally on my integrity. I hate this two-faced part of me. I guess it's just so afraid of being left out.

One approach to understanding and healing this internal compartmentalization is called Internal Family Systems Theory (IFS). It is a powerful tool for recovery from BED. Developed by Richard Schwartz, IFS is based in family systems theory and the paradigm of "multiplicity of the mind." IFS has commonalities with other theories of conceptualizing our inner world, including Freud's id, ego, and superego, and more recently, object relations theorists' concept of "internal objects." IFS concepts are also increasingly becoming part of cognitive-behavioral approaches.

While we are obviously not literally made up of many different people, IFS provides a non-pathologizing way to understand how people act from one internal "reality" one minute and a different internal "reality" the next. It seeks to describe and explain how we may feel completely able to withstand the urge to binge early in the day, but feel overwhelmed by the drive for food later on, seeming almost like two different people. IFS describes how we might feel confident and loved by our partner one minute, but then when they are late to call, quickly fear he or she might be planning to leave. It describes why we might feel body shame one day, but be able to rationalize ourselves into a binge the next.

Basically, IFS proposes our inner world is experienced as a core healthy "Self" and a number of discrete "parts," differing for each of us in both kind and number. Each part has valuable qualities and plays an important role within our psychological life. These various parts coalesce most strongly around important times and experiences in our lives, both positive and negative. When a part holds the experience of something painful or frightening, it may be forced out of its developmentally appropriate role. This is often the experience of having to be "older than our years" to survive family or cultural dysfunction. Such experiences might also include abuse or neglect, as well as the situational traumas including poverty, racism, misogyny, homophobia, or weight stigma. Parts become tasked with *surviving* instead of *thriving*. As a result, we might overdevelop one part and under-develop another.

Parts can be many ages (toddler, young child, middle-schooler, teenager, young adult), and have many characteristics within those ages. Each part can deal with the world in varying ways, some helpful, some destructive, but always trying its best to survive. When a part is holding thoughts, feelings or other somatic sensations from shameful or frightening experiences, we can become overwhelmed by their sudden appearance when triggered by an experience in the present. We have a very difficult time understanding and dealing with the emotions of these parts, especially fear, shame, and anger. We thus continue to distance from inner conflicts and, in the case of

BED, go to binge eating to numb and soothe a chaotic and frightening inner world.

> Whenever I meet new people, I am immediately back in fifth grade when I was rejected by my peers and teased for being fat. I had a group of friends one day, and then the next day, they decided to focus their teasing energy on me. I had no idea what I had done to deserve it. I was devastated. Every time now, when I don't know someone, I feel that same terror, and anticipation of shame. It makes the risk of connection overwhelming most of the time, so I stay home, where I feel safe. Alone, but safe.

> My bosses always trigger my perfectionistic middle-schooler. If the teacher liked me, it was like having an adult I could count on. When they didn't, I was alone. The best option was to be the best student, all the time. Now, when I get a new job, I'm terrified for months that I'll be "discovered" making some error, and I'll be alone again.

> Dating has been so frightening for me. I am sure every guy I meet is going to attack me. I am always armored up, even when I know in my gut it's a good guy.

The work of healing in IFS is not to eliminate a "part" but to invite the various parts' needs and feelings into awareness, begin to differentiate present from past needs, and take compassionate action as needed. Essentially, it is our healthy adult Self's job to make certain our parts are listened to, believed, and protected.

▶ THE SELF

Another key aspect of the IFS model holds that in addition to our parts, everyone has at their core a healthy adult Self. This Self is *undamaged by the experience of trauma*, and free of the cacophony of inner critic voices. When we are in Self, we feel natural, authentic, and centered. We know that our feelings and experiences are just that, *not who we are*, and possibly not even reflective of the truth.

Self is the place from which we can observe our own actions, thoughts, and feelings without becoming pulled into the sensations or the narratives they might bring. It is the energy from which we can lead and protect our own lives with the tools we have at our disposal. Self is the space we sometimes touch that feels able to let go of binge eating, to deal with whatever comes our way, and to meet loss or joy or fear with mindful, gentle compassion. Self allows us to endure uncertainty and safely navigate connection with others. It is empathetic and sympathetic, and also protective. It is accepting of what we are or have been, regardless of external judgments or our life circumstances.

If your Self energy feels elusive (or even nonexistent), you may have more sense of it when you are helping or advising others, or when you feel compassion for others' suffering. Richard Schwartz describes the Self as possessing the following list of "C" words: calmness, curiosity, clarity, compassion, confidence, creativity, courage, and connectedness. The goal of IFS work is to differentiate the Self from other younger parts, and allow the Self's innate resources to protect and to heal. While no one lives in Self energy all the time, it is an exceptionally useful tool to be able to get back to this space when we become hijacked by a scared or shame-filled younger part. Using a metaphor from meditation, the real work is not being able to meditate; it is coming back to the mat when our minds have wandered. This is true with Self energy, too; it is the "coming back" that matters most.

One of the pieces of work in recovery is to begin to separate Self from the other parts that make up the whole of who we are. This is very different from having multiple personalities. In fact, most of us can readily identify many different parts. When we are silly, joyful, feel feelings fully, or delight in sensation, we act from the openness of a child part. When we want to push back against unfair rules or "go our own way," we connect with the protective, explorative energy of the teenager in us. This is not pathology; it is the nature of maturation and incorporation of our experiences into a life narrative. In a sense, we are made up of all the ages we have ever been. IFS simply asks us to be aware and attentive to these aspects of our inner world, and see what their needs, or fears, might be.

When there is a "safe enough" developmental environment, we can remain connected to all parts of us as we develop and grow. As adults, we can tend to these various parts, hear what each may have to contribute, and navigate life from Self most of the time. We may feel child-like and vulnerable at times, or rebellious and angry at others, but we recognize these reactions as a mood or space we're in temporarily. We can recognize what is happening, and come back to Self with relative ease.

However, when a person develops BED, it is likely some parts have become distanced from conscious awareness, particularly if they carry once unacceptable fear, shame, or anger. It is only when they overwhelm our Self that we may become aware of their existence. Again, it is important to note that these parts are not the enemy, nor are they evidence of brokenness. When we think about having BED, most people (and therapies) have a tendency to see the pathology, or the places where our parts have taken over and drive destructive behaviors like binge eating. This is not pathology; it is survival.

▶ HIJACKED BY A PART

Consider times when you experienced emotions you rationally knew were out of proportion to the situation. Do you feel overwhelmed by shame and fear if you have to cancel a lunch date, or enraged if someone cuts you off in traffic? Do you ever feel completely hopeless that life will get better? Or certain that you will be alone and never find a partner? Have you ever gone rapidly from feeling like a capable adult to feeling like a frightened child or enraged teenager? Even though you are aware your reaction might not make sense, it seems impervious to rational intervention. This is how our parts carry our history with us. We react to the *present* from the voice and experience of the *past*. This is actually how we are neurologically wired to remember perceived threat. But because these experiences are to some degree out of the awareness of the Self, the energy comes out "sideways," triggered by current experiences that seem in some way similar to the original threat. We get hijacked—suddenly overwhelmed by the shame, fear, or anger still carried, unable in the moment to differentiate past from present. Life feels overwhelming, scary, enraging, or out of control. We feel anxious or depressed, or both. And our authentic, powerful Self seems nowhere to be found. It is no wonder that people with BED often begin using food early on in their lives to deal with these overwhelming feelings and sensations.

Richard Schwartz notes that when dealing with parts, "there's no shortcut around our inner barbarians." In other words, we must learn to listen to our most unwelcome parts and embrace them. If we can do so, they transform. We discover the parts about which we feel the most shame are simply afraid or hurt. When we can meet this inner world with the C's of Self, it becomes a place of safety and acceptance. We begin to experience the care that we needed all along. Binge eating becomes less and less needed as the way to seek refuge.

▶ YOUNG AND SCARED: OUR "CHILD" PARTS

Often quite active for people with BED and trauma histories are our various "child" parts. These parts needed the protection of caregivers to survive and are thus triggered to appear whenever we feel the threat of rejection, judgment, or abandonment. Child parts, when they believe they have disappointed important people, obsess over minor mistakes, feel shame intensely, and experience heightened anxiety about life in general and the certainty of loss of love and connection. Our child parts may hold the belief that we will never measure up to the demands of others, and will ultimately be alone. For people with BED, this trigger often happens around food and body shame.

> I'm always judging what I ate. And what you ate. And what everyone ate. Because people talk about it. They are vegan. Or gluten free. And they talk about how great they feel and how they went to the gym that morning or they rode their bike 45 miles. And they just need to lose 5 more pounds. And I'm sitting there trying to make myself invisible so they don't see the 50 pounds I need to lose. I don't engage. I smile nervously. I try to change the subject, sometimes. I tell myself it doesn't matter, my journey isn't their journey. But it feels connected. It feels like I'm doing something wrong, that I'm missing something. They have some gene for exercise that I don't. They have some source of energy that I don't. I have no motivation. I have no willpower. The litany in my head berates me. Constantly. I'm not doing enough, I'm not good enough, I'm not enough.

This young part is actually seeking to protect us from rejection by denouncing actions or aspects of us that others may not accept. One client of mine, for example, knew she was a lesbian early in her life. Each time she would feel attraction to another woman, she would attack herself with a barrage of insults, followed by long stretches of binge eating to subconsciously punish her body for its desires. She then told herself she was "too fat" to date so she would have a reason to not notice any interest from men. Her conservative family would have ostracized her had she not rejected her sexuality, and this shaming narrative had been corroborated by a cultural milieu of homophobia. It was not until she was 55 that she could make space for her true Self, soothe the terrified younger parts, and finally come out to a supportive community.

Another client of mine felt abandoned and betrayed when her son wanted to go see his father for his tenth birthday. She knew this was a good thing—the relationship her son enjoyed with his father signaled his adaptation to his parents' divorce, which had been tough for them all. But my client's little girl part felt like her son had chosen his dad over her. She was angry and passive aggressive toward her son on his birthday. Afterward, she felt shame and feared he would leave her. He was hurt by her behavior, and it further validated her inner story of rejection. She had a major binge the night her son was at his father's house. In truth, her son needed and loved both parents. My client was reacting to feeling rejected and abandoned by her own father many years before. She acted from that pain, losing sight of her "mom" energy who wanted to protect and cherish her boy.

Our child part's shaming is extremely persuasive. As we grow, the shaming becomes increasingly effective even when our Self knows the messages are distorted or inaccurate. For example, a client of mine talks about how she feels guilt and shame every time she cares for herself. Her young critic part runs rampant, telling her she is selfish, that she simply should not need "down time." And yet, she frequently tells her staff to take personal days to just relax and enjoy a break.

> I tell them to follow the airplane directions we all know: "put on your own oxygen mask before helping others." But if I put me first, the attack from the inside is unreal. It just doesn't seem worth the fight.

Spotting your distorted judgments and challenging them cognitively is not enough to change them. When there is a history of trauma, that young part of you won't let go of that voice easily; it is terrified to do so. *What if I am myself in the world, without my shaming critic stopping me? What if I'm my real body and my real voice? What if I listen to me? Can I be loved and OK, and be me?* Our brain has developed in ways that trigger fear when we try to challenge the status quo. Our recovery from BED is much easier when we know how to meet these parts effectively.

▶ THE REBEL PART: "JUST TRY AND STOP ME"

Many of my clients know themselves to be fighters when the going gets rough. They say things like "Nobody is telling me what to do!" or "I have trouble following rules." Many of them are quick to defend and protect others. From this part of themselves, compliance and obedience is tantamount to giving up and losing, and can be one of the backlash forces against giving into body shame and dieting.

> My "inner dieter" gets drowned out by my binge voice. When I decide to binge, the resounding thought is "Screw you, good girl, and screw you, Barbie."

> The second someone tells me something I should do, I immediately feel the need to do the opposite, even if I actually find their suggestion appealing.

> I eat food when I don't want it, when I'm not hungry, just because I *shouldn't*.

Many clients of mine have a good deal of pride in this rebel part. It holds their truth by saying no to expectations of others, and defies the rules, including the rules about eating and weight. This is not to say being in a bigger body is just about rebellion. But for some people, binge eating, and sometimes body size, can offer opportunities for communication. It can say "don't mess with me" or "something is wrong." Again, we must remember that a bigger body is not simply some psychological "cry for help." What is critical is the psychological meaning the person *attributes* to their size, not their actual body.

Such energy develops in adolescence. Especially in families where the "good kid" is the favored over authenticity, our "rebel" can be a lifeline. The rebel is often at odds with our "good kid" part, but it can also feel taxed with protecting that which the "good kid" seems bent on hiding: our unique self.

Sometimes the rebellious teen and the good kid can reach an uneasy détente in relationship to food.

> I've never had a classic all-out eat-a-whole-half-gallon-of-ice-cream-followed-by-a-bag-of-M&Ms-and-a-bucket-of-fried-chicken-type binge. My binges are more like have some crackers and cheese, then 20–30 minutes later a half a sandwich. Then a half hour later a bowl of

frozen yogurt; then later some chips and salsa. Grazing. I'm in the zone when I graze-binge. I would tell myself "I'll start my diet tomorrow" or "I will skip dinner tonight" or "I'll have to exercise extra tomorrow to make up for these extra calories." It's being "good" while being "bad."

Ultimately, both the rebel part and good kid part want the same thing: to be seen, heard, and cherished. They simply have very different approaches to achieving their goal, based on developmental abilities, family rules, and life experiences.

▶ YOUR BRAIN CAN HEAL

Neurologically speaking, we now know much more about why we can feel overwhelmed so quickly and why we might act out from a place of feeling threatened, even when threat no longer exists. Growing up, when something happens to us that is psychologically damaging and we are too powerless to stop it or to escape, we need some means by which we can endure the situation. To be able to have any sense of safety and any relationship to those in charge, we disconnect in many ways from our own experience of such events. Our brain has an innate capacity to compartmentalize, and we use it to full advantage in such situations. We detach from our sense of feeling vulnerable, damaged, and afraid. We deny, minimize, and turn away from big feelings. Then, as per our protective nature, when an experience in the present reminds us of this forgotten past, we react *from* those old feelings. Binge eating soothes these activations or flashbacks. Additionally, binge eating is a coping tool that does not require the dangers of interaction; quite to the contrary, it allows a powerful way to soothe and numb without any help from others. This is especially valuable when our relationships with others were an original source of the danger. Once survival habits (like binge eating) are repeated, they become procedurally learned—virtually automatic—and can happen with little or no conscious intention. Thus comes the feeling of being "taken over" by the drive to binge with little or no awareness as to *why* the drive arose.

▶ THE NEUROLOGY OF PROTECTION

Dan Siegel, M.D., is the founder of interpersonal neurobiology. This field of study looks at the development of the human brain and how it is shaped in particular by our early relationships. Dr. Siegel's work has focused on a part of the brain called the prefrontal cortex (PFC). Early relationships profoundly affect the PFC. When we are adequately protected and acknowledged as infants and children, our PFC teaches us to turn toward others for help in times of stress. We develop a healthy interdependence with other people, able to share with them our authentic self without shame or fear. We feel able to tolerate the conflict and loss that can happen in relationships, knowing we will still be loved by others and safe. When others are not available, we learn to self-soothe from these internalized healthy models of compassion.

As we mature, the prefrontal cortex is also responsible for creating a coherent temporal narrative of our lives, assigning meaning to events happening in the present using wisdom from similar events to those of the past. We must integrate a past event, our response to it, the effectiveness of the response, what we have learned from it, and what we might be able to do differently in the future. The prefrontal cortex creates the neural integration of the story—how we relate to our experience. With this integration, when we have been safe enough, we can step into our unfolding lives even when we are scared, trusting we will make our way.

When human development into adulthood proceeds well, the prefrontal cortex allows a person to sense their core values, to intuit what's right for them and what is not. We call this a "gut" feeling because our breath, heart, and diaphragm, via our autonomic nervous system, are physically involved. Intuition is deep, profound knowledge, below conscious processing. The prefrontal cortex integrates somatic information, emotions, cognitions, and past experience, guiding our actions and choices in the present. It also allows us to experience empathy and a sense of the interconnectedness of all life. We are then able to make choices not only for personal survival—which our amygdala critically does full-time—but for the common good. Feeling such connection fundamentally feeds us. Being good to ourselves and to others feels good, right, and true.

When psychological danger exists with any regularity, the PFC is unable to do its job effectively. We do not develop a cohesive story of our lives; our inner world is chaotic or unclear, and we have little sense of our own needs and feelings. We tend to distrust others to be helpful or supportive when we need it most. Our shame voice keeps us from taking the risk to reach out. Our Self is overpowered by old demons, unable to address shame and fear when it arises. We obsess about the health of our relationships, we feel unlovable and unacceptable. Food, not connection to Self or others, is further reinforced as the safest option to soothe and disconnect from pain.

It is essential to remember our life circumstances and cultural milieu may add significant hurdles to the work of healing from BED. We cannot change weight stigma, racism, homophobia, ableism or poverty by rewiring our brains' reactions. However, we can become an advocate for ourselves, and work for change on a larger scale. We are less likely to accept discrimination or believe shame messages to be true, and more likely to challenges institutions that systematically harm us or others, when we have done our own healing work. We become more tolerant of those who are different from us, and better able to see from someone else's perspective without feeling threatened.

▶ THE TRUTH ABOUT EMOTIONS

Emotions of all kinds are natural—even when they are big, unexpected, out of proportion, or not "sensible." Though they may seem so at times, *our emotions are not who we are*, but only our reactions to our inner and outer environments and our experiences. They ebb and they flow. They can be activated by the experience of the moment, or by a memory, or both at the same time. They may or may not reflect the truth of the present moment. They get easier to handle with practice, moving toward them instead of acting as though they are a danger. And allowing them is essential to changing our relationship with food.

Emotions are neurologically driven waves of sensation that signal your body—through the insula—to pay attention and possibly mobilize to act. The insula reads the physiological state of the body and generates the experience of "feelings," which bring about actions to keep the body in a state of internal balance. For example, anger may make us aware of an injustice or a violation of our boundaries. When angry, we tense up and may prepare for conflict. If we're afraid, we become more alert and hyper-vigilant, scan our surroundings, and may prepare to flee if need be. In sadness and grief, we contract in, becoming smaller, child-like. If we feel shame, we collapse, withdraw, disconnect, hide, and try desperately not to draw attention. All emotions trigger reactions—sometimes our reactions protect us and contribute to resilience in recovery, sometimes not. We do not have the power to control our emotional reactions. Thankfully, however, we do have the power to change our *reactions to our emotions* to serve us better.

Emotions are lived in our *body*, not our mind. While they may be accompanied by thoughts, emotions are completely somatic reactions. We each experience the sensations of emotions differently; for some people, fear lives mostly in the gut, for others in their neck or back. Anger may come in a clenched jaw, or shallow breathing. Joy may be experienced as energy and excitement for some, and a sense of peace and relaxation for others. Our emotions are a significant source of information about both inner and outer worlds, and aid us greatly in determining the best course of action. Until our emotions can be met and managed with compassion and curiosity, there can be no wholeness, no real sense of well-being, and no solid sense of self-worth. The good news is that we are actually *hardwired* to do this very well, even when we have survived considerable psychological or physical damage. The idea that feelings can overwhelm us, drive us crazy, never end, or are somehow shameful, are messages from hurt, often young, parts of us. It is the *fear* of the emotion, not the emotion itself, that causes our avoidance. In truth, even though it may not seem so, our adult Self can more than handle our feelings.

For most people with BED, our families and the culture have not made it comfortable to express emotion. Pete Walker, a psychotherapist specializing in recovery from childhood trauma, writes about it this way:

> Nowhere, not in the deepest recesses of the self, or in the presence of one's closest friends, is the average person allowed to have and explore any number of normal emotional states. Anger, depression, envy, sadness, fear, distrust, are all as normal a part of life as bread and flowers and streets; yet they have become ubiquitously avoided and shameful human experiences. How tragic this is, for all of these emotions have enormously important and healthy functions in a wholly integrated psyche.

When we learn early on we must detach from certain feelings, we tend to act to keep the disconnect going even when any danger is long past. Our feelings can thus seem inexplicable, indefensible, frightening, or "crazy."

Unfortunately, without having access to the spectrum of our emotions, we are deprived of the ability to notice when something is unfair, abusive, or neglectful (not to mention joyful, exciting, or desirable). For example, people who do not feel their sadness often do not know when they are being treated unfairly. Those who cannot feel angry or fearful are often in danger of allowing harm without protest. The very thing that historically was in our best interests now renders us vulnerable and less able to keep ourselves psychologically, and sometimes physically, safe.

▶ HIJACKED BY THE PAST

When we have an emotional reaction in the present moment that reactivates old shame and fear narratives, we are being "hijacked" by the past. Our brain is literally behaving as though we are back in time. Until we are consciously aware of this occurring, we can do little to intervene. We may experience a rush of shame or fear or anger out of proportion to the situation. The old stories from our youngest parts—I am not lovable, I will be alone, I am not good enough—operate at the same time as present experiences unfold. Our brain responds to the *old* threat of danger, forgetting we are here, now, grown up. The cycle of a hijack goes something like this:

- ▶ At a time in your development when you are dependent, you have experiences with important caregivers that threaten your sense of safety in the world.

- ▶ Your amygdala responds to this experience with "Warning! Danger!" You feel fear/anxiety.

- ▶ Over time, a conclusion of self-blame happens to explain this experience and thus mediate the fear: "I must have caused/deserved this." Shame results.

- ▶ This response is reinforced each time a similar experience occurs and the links become more and more entrenched.

- ▶ Something happens in your present life that reminds you of this old experience; we may or may not consciously feel the fear and shame.

▶ The amygdala responds as though the same threat has reoccurred now; you thus experience your inner world somatically and emotionally as though you are currently in that very circumstance, *at that age*.

▶ The insula signals for you to get away from this experience immediately, activating the fight/flight/freeze/fawn system.

▶ The urge to binge is activated—it is becomes "knee jerk" over time; the brain circuit to binge becomes locked firmly into place (it is now "procedurally learned").

▶ You binge eat (for most people, binge eating is a "flight" response).

▶ Dopamine is released and you feel temporarily soothed (this rush of dopamine paves the neural pathway for binge eating).

▶ Your brain records binge eating as "effective" and the circuit is further reinforced.

▶ You feel shame and fear (of weight gain) because of the binge.

▶ Your "fight" part tends to activate with the critic voice, shaming us into another swearing off/diet to save the day.

A few examples may help make this clearer. One client of mine described a sense of panic at the idea of cleaning out old papers and magazines from her house. Despite her husband's frustration (and hers too), every time she approached the task, she felt overwhelmed with fear and shame. As she and I examined this reaction, it became clear she reacted from a young part, from dangers of early childhood. She remembered the erratic nature of her mom's rage; her mother blamed her for all kinds of things she could not possibly have caused. My client's "good kid" part told her it must somehow be her fault that her mother was so angry—after all, she could not consider her mother might be wrong or dangerous, as my client's survival was dependent on her. This old fear and shame was triggered by the risk of throwing things away in the present. Suppose she threw away the one thing she might need, the one thing that would allow her to get it right? Throwing something away felt dangerous. So, she avoided the task at all costs, and continued to hoard objects that one day might save her from rejection. In the present day, even thinking about the idea of clearing out these objects activated a hijack, and my client would find herself, instead of making progress on the reorganization, grazing through the cupboards for something sweet.

Another client feels enraged when her husband forgets some insights she told him from her therapy sessions. Her mother used to pass out from drinking when she really needed her as a young girl. Her husband's forgetfulness feels much like when her mother would simply emotionally disappear. Her fight response comes on instantly, and full force, forgetting how deeply he cares about her recovery, and she is unable to let him know her need for his attention. The situation ends inevitably with shame, a familiar sense of being all alone, and a binge.

▶ THE SECOND PRACTICE: POWR

Thankfully, our brain has the ability to pause and notice when something arouses our attention. We can actually meet our experience with gentle awareness and regulate our emotions to tolerable levels, lessening the need to go to food. We can then assess what is *actually* happening, and act wisely to care for ourselves. Response flexibility, according to Dan Siegel, is the fulcrum for change and healing. The more flexible we can be and the more options we can identify, the more resilient we will be. This is especially critical when living in a world that can be oppressive, and where shaming messages are ubiquitous. Over time, we can respond to these hijack moments by moving *toward* the experience with focus and intention instead of fleeing. We can literally influence our brain to change when it activates our threat response. We can unlearn old narratives, and stay with ourselves more and more often without needing to escape into a binge. We can advocate effectively and compassionately on our own behalf in our relationships, and in our culture at large.

In my practice with BED clients, I use what we know about the healing ability of the brain to help my clients become aware of when they are hijacked by a younger part, learning how to get back to their adult, in-the-present Self. Clients come away feeling safer, more powerful, and much less in need of escape. I use a process I call POWR to help clients regulate back to what trauma therapists call the "window of tolerance," where emotions are present but not overwhelming. It is this process, repeated over and over, that gently allows us to rewire the way we react to our inner world and to the world around us. We become more resilient, better able to handle emotions, and more compassionate. As we heal in this way, we are also increasingly able to care for ourselves and our bodies well, connect with safe others, and meet authentic desires as we are able. In the words of one client:

> When faced with discouraging, shaming, or scary perceived "messages" from whatever sources (internal or external), I am learning to stop what I am doing, take a deep breath, name the invading message, and consider very carefully how I interpret it in the moment. Gradually, I am learning to take my own side in a conflict. I'm also learning each stone we loosen from that old protective wall that keeps us covered is worth every minute. My voice keeps getting stronger.

▶ BUILDING AWARENESS OF HIJACK

When we are hijacked by a young part, like our "good girl" or "rebel," three changes take place. We *believe the worldview* of that part, we *feel the emotions* of that part, and we *act* from that part's abilities. We lose track of our wise adult Self. A couple of examples might help clarify this point. A client of mine owns and manages an apartment building. Whenever she gets a call about a problem from a tenant, she feels overwhelming fear and shame. Somehow, she believes in that moment any problem with the building is a reflection on her worth and value—nothing should ever go wrong. Her "flight" response activates, and she avoids returning the call. She feels a bit of her rebel, as she is angry at the interruption and activation. In these moments, my client has been hijacked by her young "good girl" self, forgetting temporarily that her safety and lovability are in no way connected to a problem with building maintenance. These calls almost always triggered a binge episode.

Another client of mine felt absolutely trapped in a loveless, disconnected marriage. Whenever her normal life Self would begin to long for something different, a young part of her felt terrified that she could not be safe without this marriage. She would be back in her eight-year-old world, seeing her mother sink into a profound depression upon the death of her father. Her mother literally stopped functioning, unable to care for herself or my client, or her baby sister. My client was terrified and alone, uncertain she would survive having essentially lost both of her caregivers.

It is in times such as this, when the urge to binge (or when emotions of any kind) seem overwhelming, that POWR is a useful tool. There are four steps to the POWR process—Pause into presence, Open and allow, Wisely consider, and Respond with care. Please remember that POWR is a recovery tool for dealing with the ongoing after effects of very difficult experiences. As such, if you have a trauma history and BED, it is likely important to be in treatment with a BED trauma-trained therapist when working to implement the POWR process. Let's go through each step in turn.

▶ PAUSE INTO PRESENCE

Pausing into presence sounds simple enough, but it can be a revolutionary act. After all, having BED implies some kind of frequent disconnection from our inner world. Think about how difficult it can be to look into your own eyes in the mirror. Or to read your journal entries, or look at old photos, without feeling a sense of vulnerability or shame. So much of the relationship we have with ourselves is likely about avoidance or damage control. Thus, this process of pausing far from easy.

Although it may sound incredible, we should *naturally* feel at home in our own skin most of the time, safe with our thoughts, feelings, and sensations. We should be able to be our (and our body's) best friend. For people struggling with BED, things are far from this. Thus, a big part of POWR is about working on developing compassion for all you have done to survive, including binge eating, and about meeting the real needs you have in the present. It is about developing the ability to be your own advocate and ally.

Another term for presence is "the felt sense." According to Peter Levine, our "felt sense" is the awareness of our ever-changing sensory/energetic/emotional landscape. The felt sense shifts our focus from actions and things happening outside us in the world to our present, internal experience. It is where we can best reconnect with that wise Self when we become hijacked. There is no "right answer" in the felt sense, no expectation about what you might, or should, feel. It is simply *bringing attention* to right here, right now. For most people with BED, there is very little non-judgmental awareness about our inner experience. We assess, resolve, or try to change most every-thing about ourselves from our scared and ashamed parts.

> Historically, I walk, talk, and think so quickly that other people remark on it. What drives my speed is not just that I love to move and I have lots of things I want to do. What drives me is that I believe there's a crisis developing—always! And, that speed is of utmost importance to avert disaster. I never stop and see if there is *actually* any threat. I just assume there is and keep moving.

The felt sense, the true domain of the Self, invites you to simply *notice* your inner experience, meeting whatever you find with curiosity and compassion. From this place of gentle awareness, you can assess your desire for food and movement, for rest, for connection, or time to be alone. Even if you don't (or can't) do what your felt sense asks, you may still learn something about yourself from the experience. And simply seeing ourselves without judgment intrinsically heals shame and lessens fear.

While you may well be afraid of what you will discover when you pause and look inward, the far greater danger is in *not* looking. When you back away from inner experience, you *confirm that your fears are trustworthy and real*, and that you cannot protect yourself. You continue the belief that past tigers remain, unchanged. The emotional need for escape into binge eating is reinforced, and goes again unchallenged. Pausing into presence is actually about stepping back into Self, and moving toward vulnerable parts when they need your care the most.

> When I think about how well I can step up to the plate and support others at their most vulnerable, when they feel the most devastated, I remember I might be able to offer that support to myself, too. It's not that it isn't there; it's just that I didn't know such compassion was also meant for me.

Pausing is the first step toward knowing what is *actually occurring in the moment*, separating the present from the old stories we tell ourselves. It is coming to see we can handle whatever we find, be it from memory or in the present.

Disconnection from ourselves, while once a necessity to survive, can put us in harm's way by masking *real* dangers in the present. Pausing helps us recognize when we might need to be our own best friend and protector.

> I was full of shame about an interaction I'd had with one of my students that day. I was sure I had lost all credibility in her eyes, and did not deserve to be a professor, much less a dean. I was feeling failure and fear—just as I did years ago with my judgmental father—when suddenly I noticed an amazing sunset out my window. I was taken aback by its beauty and color. My shame and fear, in that moment, were suspended by simply appreciating the beauty of nature. That was all it took for me to realize my shame was driven by a young, scared part of myself. It was not actually in response to my life *now*. I knew my father was wrong about me. He had had his own heart broken, and all he could see was his own shame because he was never good enough. I needed to learn to come back into my adult wisdom if I was going to address and soothe this recurring shame storm. My father was not an accurate judge of my ability. Nor is my "good girl" part. I am capable, even if I make a mistake. I didn't get to this place in my career by accident or by fraud. I got here by hard work, skill, and support from colleagues. I deserve to be here. I just lost track of that for a moment. I was 10 again.

Pausing creates the space for an accurate assessment of what's happening in the moment, and what—if anything—you need to do to care for yourself. Pausing sets the stage for the remaining steps of POWR; it allows for gentle awareness of your world from a space of safety, instead of fear or shame.

When you feel hijacked by a younger part or a big feeling, one powerful tool to initiate a pause is your breath. Meditation teachers have long known the power of focused breathing. It helps us get back to ground, center ourselves, and critically, helps bring our prefrontal cortex back online. Focused breathing allows the parasympathetic nervous system (PNS) to activate our natural "brake," ratcheting down our threat response. It helps bring you back to the present, to the window of tolerance, able to address what is *actually occurring in the moment*. I have found "square breathing" to be a helpful technique.

In square breathing, each step is one side of an imaginary square. To begin, bring your focus in. Close your eyes. Take a moment to feel your body's contact with the earth, whether standing, seated, or lying down. Try to allow the melting of any tightness in your body. Then, breathe in to the count of five, hold for a count of five, exhale for a count of five, and rest for a count of five, thus making the "square" of four steps. Repeat five times. With each exhale, imagine stress drifting out and away. Then, notice your experience. What is happening in your body? Do you feel any sensations? Any emotions? Do you feel the drive to get back to thinking/worrying? Allow these sensations for a minute or two, and notice what happens to them as time passes.

There are many techniques and meditations to focus your breathing. You may wish to try others and see what calms you most. Or, you may wish to add a meditation component to your breathing. For example, you might bring to mind someone/something you love with each inhale. Or you might consider something for which you feel gratitude as you complete each square. Some people bring to mind a favorite color or sensation instead. Over time, you will likely develop strategies of your own, or different strategies for different needs. Try square breathing when you feel stuck or disconnected, too. Try making a week-long commitment to pause at the same time each day. See if anything changes for you. Pausing is best done with conscious intent. Over time, it becomes a gentle, healing practice.

Remember, you may struggle with any "practice" as though it were a diet or another rule, another "should." When you feel this way, allow the feeling to arise. It is here for good reason, and needs to be met gently and heard. You need to address the part of you that may feel trapped by using the POWR process. After all, you have most likely been molding yourself to the demands of others, or the rules of a diet, for a very long time. Now, though, any intention you set can be a decision completely under your control. You can simply offer yourself the *opportunity* to try a breathing technique, and decide if you wish to do so in that moment.

Another practice to pause into presence I have found helpful I refer to as "calling on love." Place one hand on your heart and one in the center of your abdomen. (If touching your abdomen triggers body shame, place your hand only on your heart until you feel ready to do both.) Breathe gently and deeply, filling your belly. Imagine the breath moving into your heart and filling you with a warm sense of goodness, safety, and acceptance. Call to mind a moment of being with someone who loves you unconditionally, someone with whom you feel completely safe. This might be a partner or a parent, a good friend, a trusted teacher. It could be your therapist, your grandmother, a third-grade teacher, a beloved pet. As you remember feeling safe and loved, see if you can feel the sensations in your body. Savor this feeling of warmth, safety, trust, and love in your body. When that feeling is steady, let go of the image and allow yourself to bask in the feeling for a moment.

Ultimately, pausing into presence is about creating space to gently sort out, in the present moment, what is happening before taking action. Anything that allows you to step back into your powerful adult Self is useful; you will find your own paths to get there. My clients over the years have developed many pause techniques to slow down and reconnect, including reciting a favorite poem to themselves, singing a comforting song, or even simply reciting the alphabet backwards! From there, they can do square breathing or any centering strategy they like best. Anything that bring you back to the here and now gently, works.

▶ OPEN AND ALLOW

To "open and allow" means simply noticing, with curiosity and without judgment, your experience *in the moment*. What is happening right now somatically, emotionally, and cognitively? What is happening outside, in your immediate environment?

Consider the step of open and allow to be something like watching a movie about your experience of the moment. Open and allow asks you to notice— without judgment and with curiosity—what is happening *without trying to change it*. What are you physically feeling in your body? What are your emotions (there may well be more than one)? What are your thoughts? What is happening around you? When you pause and become fully present, you can take stock of your situation and identify what you feel. Pausing into presence and opening and allowing puts you solidly inside the window of tolerance. You are here, now, and not there, then. Many of my clients find it helpful to actually name (aloud, if possible) their experience of the moment. Saying it helps to activate our prefrontal cortex, further stepping into Self. We feel calmer and more able to tolerate what we are experiencing.

Self-compassion is an essential ingredient to be able to open and allow our experience. Kristin Neff, Ph.D., in her book *Self Compassion*, describes compassion for others, something we can often more easily access, this way:

> First, to have compassion for others you must notice that they are suffering. Second, compassion involves feeling moved by others' suffering so that your heart responds to their pain (the word compassion literally means to "suffer with"). When this occurs, you feel warmth, caring, and the desire to help the suffering person in some way. Having compassion also means that you offer understanding and kindness to others when they fail or make mistakes, rather than judging them harshly. Finally, when you feel compassion for another (rather than mere pity), it means that you realize that suffering, failure, and imperfection is part of the shared human experience.

This is also the exact process for *self*-compassion. You must, first and foremost, notice you are indeed suffering. You need your own attention and help, and are as deserving of it as anyone else.

There is mounting clinical research suggesting self-compassion is a critical ingredient in building resilient recovery. Recovery is strongest, according to a growing body of research, when our life story is complete, coherent, emotionally congruent, and told from a *sympathetic perspective*. When you acknowledge the harm you have experienced (and may continue to experience), and tell the truth about its impact, you get to the root of your relationship with food. It is empowering to fully understand the significance of childhood experiences—to realize how the uncertainty, panic, toxic shame, helplessness, or hopelessness you presently experience are emotional and somatic reenactments from childhood. Compassion for yourself provides what you missed in the past—receiving empathy when in pain, instead of contempt or abandonment. This change toward compassion literally *rewires the brain*. You move closer to self-awareness and further away from the old stories of shame and fear. Thus we can love ourselves, and ultimately others, well.

To open and allow, label your emotions aloud if possible, and notice how your body communicates those feelings to you. "I am angry right now" or "I am feeling sad." How do you know? What physical sensations tell you this? Giving a name to the emotional experience activates the parasympathetic nervous system—the brake to the fight/flight/freeze/fawn reaction. You bring your Self wisdom back online by bearing witness to what happens and stepping out of the experience itself; you can *notice* your response. You step back a bit and observe. This is a critical part of healing old wounds. You will come to see *you are not your pain*, and that you have different resources and skills now. You can protect yourself from danger, or you can call in safe people to help.

For my clients who did not grow up with attuned, empathic caregivers or are not sure how to hear their own compassionate Self voice, I suggest a guided imagery exercise I call "The Board of Directors." Begin with square breathing, allowing yourself to be present in this moment. Then bring to mind a safe space familiar to you, or create one. In the center of this private and completely secure space, notice a large table with one empty chair on one side, and a number of empty chairs opposite. Sit down in the one seat and allow yourself to relax.

In the chairs opposite will be seated your Board of Directors: people, characters, creatures, or animals, even objects, real or imagined, who will advise you on how to care for and protect yourself. Turn away from the table and close your eyes for a moment while your Board enters. Take a few deep breaths. Open your eyes and turn back to face the table. Who entered the room and took a seat? Are they familiar? Are they real or fictitious? Animal or human? What does each bring to you? Ask them for their guidance going forward. Ask if they have anything to tell you right now. Is there anyone you would like to add? Feel free to do so. You can call on any or all of these figures as you learn along the way how to best hear, and respond to, your inner world.

One rather lovely thing I have discovered over years of doing this exercise: your board members are actually a reflection of your adult Self who has been waiting to emerge. These Board members came to mind because they are mirrors of who you already are. That is why they appeal to you. If you try this exercise, I would offer one important caveat: is how you *imagine* the people or creatures on your Board, and not who they actually *are*, that matters. It is your version of them that will help lead the way.

The POWR step of open and allow is not about making things better, or making pain go away. It is about meeting your in-the-moment experience *whatever it may be.* "This allows us to hold ourselves in love and connection, giving ourselves the support and comfort needed to bear the pain, while providing the optimal conditions for growth and transformation," according to Dr. Neff. In other words, when you allow yourself to feel what you feel without judgment, you can allow pain to pass, and change to happen.

If you are disconnected from your emotions, it may be difficult to identify and label them. One suggestion is to create a feelings catalog. When you are relatively safe and calm, give yourself some space to explore the experience of your emotional language. Consider a feeling you'd like to identify. Perhaps sadness, or anger, or joy. Sit comfortably, close your eyes if you feel comfortable doing so, and try a few square breaths. Remind yourself this is only an exercise, you are safe, and there is no judgment about what you discover. This is all about getting to know yourself better. Bring to mind a time when you likely experienced the feeling you wish to explore. Choose an event where the feeling is clear, but also manageable. For example, if you wish to explore sadness, you might bring to mind saying goodbye when a friend moved away. Or if the feeling is joy, you might wish to recall walking on a lovely forest path. Try to bring the experience of an emotion to mind. Where were you? What sounds and smells were there? What time of year? Who else was there? Allow the experience to unfold, and as you do, pay close attention to what happens in your body. Remember feelings are experienced *somatically*. Notice what sensations happen. Any tightening or loosening in your muscles? What does your brow do? Your jaw? Your hands and feet? Do you notice any changes in body temperature? Heart rate? Keep bringing compassionate curiosity to the experience. Do you notice any judgments about what you are experiencing? Does this emotion feel identified with the good or rebel parts? Or another part? Simply take note of your observations. Stay present with it for as long as you wish, knowing you are safe. If at any time you wish to stop, simply open your eyes. When you feel like you have all the information you can gather, come back to the present slowly. Become aware of the chair underneath you, the air on your skin, and especially any bodily changes as you transition back to the present. When you are ready, take a few square breaths and open your eyes. See if you can feel gratitude for your attempt to heal in this way. When you are ready, and if it appeals to you, consider writing in a log book or journal what you experienced for this emotion.

You may wish to try this exercise with a variety of feelings and compare the nuanced differences in your body. When you can label feelings in the body, you can deal with them as sensations, allowing them to pass through without knocking you out of the window of tolerance.

It may be helpful to start your feelings exploration with an awareness exercise I learned from Charlene Bell Tosi, a dear friend and founder of Woman Within International, which offers retreats worldwide for women to heal from old narratives and reclaim their true voices. Char taught me a check-in technique called PIES (Physical, Intellectual, Emotional, and Spiritual). It involves a brief systematic assessment of your in the moment experience to build the muscle of awareness. Each time you do PIES you enhance the connection between awareness and self-compassion. I typically suggest people do this exercise a few times per day. It should take no more than a couple of minutes. It might help to set an alarm on your phone or computer to help remind you to do it.

To do the PIES check-in, go somewhere quiet if possible. Start with a few square breaths. Remind yourself that if you hear any judgments about what you discover in this check-in, you will notice them and allow them to float by, like leaves on water. Then, begin with a brief body scan of your physical presence. What do you notice about your body right now? Sensations of tension or looseness? Temperature? Fatigue? Energy? Does your body need anything from you right now? Next, the intellectual dimension as you check in with your thoughts. What is their content? Do they feel complete or fragmented? Are they about the present, the past, or both? Do they feel repetitive or obsessive, or are they flowing and easy? Next, what emotions are you feeling at the moment, if any? How can you tell? Are they triggering any fear or shame? Is there anything you need to do with your emotions right now, or do they just need to simply be? And finally, do a spiritual check. How is your "spirit" (meaning your overall sense of yourself and the world around you)? How do you feel about you and your world right at the moment? Peaceful? Uncertain? It is helpful to note too if you have any reactions to the process itself. And remember to meet what you find with the gentlest voice you can muster. There are no right answers here, only observation and the chance to strengthen your muscle of self-compassion.

▶ **WISELY CONSIDER**

> Be the witness of your thoughts.
>
> —Buddhist Proverb

Once you have opened and allowed yourself to witness your own emotional, cognitive, and body experience, you need to interpret your reactions. Because you are self-aware thanks to that prefrontal cortex, you are able to look at your responses to things, and with intent, gradually and gently effect change (or decide not to). You can allow yourself to notice the patterns of your responses, and connect them to your old narratives of shame and fear.

In wisely considering, begin by asking yourself this question: What is the story I'm telling myself that triggered this big feeling/reaction? These stories may be hiding underneath the specifics of the story of the moment. They are typically very global statements, all-or-nothing in nature, and ultimately, frightening. They come from old experiences and, as such, are based in the limited wisdom of our young part's understanding of the world and our place in it. For many with BED, these stories may center on body shame. If that is your current fear, what is underneath? Ask yourself: What am I telling myself will happen if my body is unacceptable in this situation?

Some common underlying backstories include:

▶   I am incompetent (not good enough, inept, ineffectual, useless)

▶   I am defective (damaged, broken, a mistake, flawed)

▶   I am dirty (soiled, ugly, unclean, impure, filthy, disgusting)

▶   I am unwanted (unseen, uncherished)

▶   I am pitiful (contemptible, miserable, insignificant)

▶   I am nothing (worthless, invisible, unnoticed, empty)

▶   I will be alone

▶   I will not survive

Try to take notice when these narratives are at play. Such underlying shame-based beliefs are the most powerful drivers of binge eating episodes.

> Today, I was working at my new job. It is a big promotion, and I am absolutely terrified to be found out as a fraud. Somehow, I'm sure I got here under false pretenses. Good things aren't supposed to happen to me. And if they do, I'm sure they will end in the catastrophe of someone seeing the real truth about me. I have been anxious and jumpy since I got this

promotion. It's exactly like it was growing up. The good work is expected, but the failures are the focus. I always feel on the edge of being judged.

It can help to understand what's happening if you ask "What age do I feel in this narrative?" Sometimes, this allows the opportunity to connect a specific time or memory. Knowing this can help you respond effectively.

I found myself being really judgmental about a presenter at our writing conference last week. How could she look like that? Frumpy, messy, fat. How could she possibly stand there and seem to be OK with herself? I was furious about it! Then, I realized that this was something I was *never* allowed to do. I was not angry with this woman; I was sad and hurt for my little girl. I never had such freedom to not worry about my appearance, and inside, I still don't.

Other common narratives might be:

- ▶ Feeling joy or peace will make me vulnerable to loss

- ▶ If I allow a certain feeling (like grief or rage), it will overcome me

- ▶ If I allow my pain, I will be stuck in it or go mad

- ▶ I will be rejected if I am emotional

- ▶ If I do not control myself (and others), I will be in danger

- ▶ If others are unhappy or unsafe, I must intervene or I am unsafe

- ▶ I am lucky to have any connection to someone at all

I am always assuming people are staring at my body, and making judgments about everything I'm doing. I feel so exposed all the time for being out of control. I am always waiting to be yelled at for looking the way I do. Now, I am terrified for my daughter. She is a big kid, and I want to put her on a diet so she won't be vulnerable the way I was.

I always make sure I give the other person's problems more room in a conversation. If I take up too much space, I will be selfish and messy to deal with. People won't stick around for that.

The more able we are to identify these powerful backstories, the better able we are to recognize why they are there: they are not factual, but the lessons our much younger selves took away from the experiences in order to survive. And even though they may absolutely *feel* true, *feelings are not facts.* They are, in this case, reactions to the very scary and painful stories we came to believe a long time ago. And even if our family or our cultural or situational milieu continue to feed us these shame-based narratives, we can now decide what, and whom, to believe.

▶ RESPOND WITH CARE

This final part of POWR is perhaps most unfamiliar. By responding with care, you give yourself the opportunity to meet your long-standing need for compassion and gentleness, and take care of yourself in the present moment. This is how you heal, and how your brain can learn a new normal in the world. It can be important to remember that *taking care of yourself will probably feel wrong.* It may seem selfish, silly, shameful, or even dangerous. Allow these feelings, and consider using the POWR process with them, too. Desire for self-care was probably best avoided historically, so this may be very new territory.

Surprisingly, our needs are often very basic. We might simply need some reassurance that the old narratives are inaccurate, we are OK now, and safe connection is possible and even abundant in the world. We might need to hear that something bad that happened was not our fault, or does not change our worth and value. We might need to know we will survive loss or pain, or not having something we desire. Or that cultural judgments about our body, gender, color, or sexual orientation are about others' fears, not about truth. We may need to reach out to someone, set a limit in a relationship, or let something go. It takes time and practice to learn to care for yourself effectively. It may not be clear what you really need. Keep asking.

> I have chosen to face off with this enigmatic question: what would you like? It's unpleasant, even painful to answer that question. Because I don't have any idea. I have to really work at it to find even a "nice try" answer. I feel like wriggling out of the situation. "Let me go!" I don't want to take the time. I'm embarrassed that I don't know the

answer. The shaming voices inside begin. *Are you kidding me? How old are you? How can you not know this?* There is shame in every direction.

Give yourself time and space to learn your needs; it is critical to long-term recovery. This can be an opportune time to enlist your Board of Directors and ask what each of them might suggest.

> I am always so sure people will leave. If I feel I said something stupid, I'm sure their love for me will change immediately. So, I have learned what I need to hear most of all is that love is deeper than words, that love can't be undone by being silly or not knowing something.

You might ask yourself: What do I need right now? You know it is probably not food (unless you are hungry), but you do need to decipher what the real need might be. It is imperative not to judge the answer, no matter what. It might be simply witnessing and releasing old feelings. You may need to cry, to yell, to write, to run, to stretch, to draw. You may need to be still and breathe. You may need to stop, to rest, to allow something in, or let something go. You may need a break. Do you need to set boundaries with someone? Challenge something? Accept something? Ask for something? Do you need to just be present with not knowing for now?

▶ RESPONDING WITH THE CARE OF CONNECTION

While self-care is critical to recovery, we also need to challenge messages about worth and lovability by connection with others who are safe and supportive. According to a recent study (Holt-Lunstad, Smith, & Layton, 2010), data suggest that individuals with adequate social relationships have a 50 percent greater likelihood of survival compared to those with poor or insufficient social relationships. The magnitude of this effect is comparable with quitting smoking, and it exceeds many well-known risk factors for mortality. Unfortunately for people with BED, one of the scariest things you can ask yourself to do is connect with others, and risk exposure of who you truly are.

Social anxiety is very common in BED. Being with others involves significant emotional work, work for which many of us have a limited toolbox. When you feel an almost constant assessment of your performance, or feel easily hurt or angered in interaction with others, it can be extremely difficult to get connection needs met. My first therapist showed me how to safely take risks and set boundaries in relationships with others by allowing me to try things with her and find my voice. I learned being authentic actually made the connection with my therapist *stronger and safer*. Without this safe step, I would have had a much longer path to healing.

Check and see if you need connection of some kind. Even if it feels too dangerous to allow that connection to happen just yet, see if you can simply acknowledge the longing. If it feels like a manageable risk, consider with whom you would like to connect, and what you might like to feel from the interaction. Is this person able to offer that? Or is someone else a better option?

Ultimately, it is most important to remember that binge eating has been a successful attempt to survive, to stay safe, and to soothe when there was little else available. BED is not about a lack of willpower, a weakness, or a defect. You have made it to the point of being able to look forensically at your relationship with food, and begin to allow your whole story to emerge. With this newfound voice comes more confidence and compassion for yourself and others. And finally, the power to call your body your own. It is to hearing and honoring your body's amazing wisdom that we now turn.

▶ BIBLIOGRAPHY

Anderson, F., Schwartz, R., & Sweezy, M. (2017). *Internal family systems skill training manual: Trauma-informed treatment for anxiety, depression, PTSD, & substance abuse.* Eau Claire, WI: PESI Publishing & Media.

Badenoch, B. (2017). *The heart of trauma: Healing the embodied brain in the context of relationships.* New York, NY: W. W. Norton & Company, Inc.

Brach, T. (2004). *Radical acceptance: Embracing your life with the heart of a Buddha.* New York, NY: Bantam.

Courtois, C. A. (2014). *It's not you, it's what happened to you: Complex trauma and treatment.* Long Beach, CA: Elements Behavioral Health.

Craig, A. D. (2009). How do you feel—now? The anterior insula and human awareness. *Nature Reviews Neuroscience, 10*(1), 59–70. Retrieved from http://doi.org/10.1038/nrn2555.

Fisher, J. (2017). *Healing the fragmented selves of trauma survivors: Overcoming internal self-alienation.* New York, NY: Routledge.

Ford, J. D., & Courtois, C. A. (Eds.). (2015). *Treating complex traumatic stress disorders in children and adolescents: Scientific foundations and therapeutic models.* New York, NY: The Guilford Press.

Goulding, R., & Schwartz, R. C. (1995). *The mosaic mind: Empowering the tormented selves of child abuse survivors.* New York, NY: W. W. Norton & Company, Inc.

Graham, L. (2013). *Bouncing back: Rewiring your brain for maximum resilience and well-being.* Novato, CA: New World Library Publishing.

Holt-Lunstad, J., Smith, T. B., & Layton, J. B. (2010). *Social relationships and mortality risk: A meta-analytic review. PLOS Med Publishing, 7*(7), e1000316.

Neff, K. (2015). *Self-compassion: The proven power of being kind to yourself.* New York, NY: William Morrow Paperbacks.

Ogden, P., & Fisher, J. (2015). *Sensorimotor psychotherapy: Interventions for trauma and attachment.* New York, NY: W. W. Norton & Company, Inc.

Orsborn, C. (2010). *The art of resilience: One hundred paths to wisdom and strength in an uncertain world,* New York, NY: Three Rivers Press, New York.

Potter-Efron, R., & and Potter-Efron, P. (1989). *Letting go of shame: Understanding how shame affects your life.* Center City, MN: Hazelden Publishing.

Schore, A. N. (2003a). *Affect regulation and the repair of the self* (Norton series on interpersonal neurobiology). New York, NY: W. W. Norton & Company, Inc.

Schore, A. N. (2003b). *Affect dysregulation and disorders of the self.* New York, NY: W. W. Norton & Company, Inc.

Schwartz, R. C. (1997). *Internal family systems therapy.* New York, NY: The Guilford Press.

Siegel, D. (2001). *The developing mind: How relationships and the brain interact to shape who we are.* New York, NY: The Guilford Press.

Siegel, D. (2010). *Mindsight: The new science of personal transformation.* New York, NY: Bantam.

Tosi, C. B. (2012). *Discover your woman within: Journey to wholeness.* Tosi and Associates.

van der Kolk, B. A. (2015). *The body keeps the score: Brain, mind, and body in the healing of trauma.* New York, NY: Penguin Books.

Walker, P. (2013). *Complex PTSD from surviving to thriving: A guide and map for recovering from childhood trauma.* Charleston, SC: CreateSpace Independent Publishing Platform.

Walker, P. (2015). *The Tao of fully feeling.* Charleston, SC: CreateSpace Independent Publishing Platform.

Williams, M. (1958). *The velveteen rabbit.* New York, NY: Doubleday.

Winnicott, D. W. (1990). *Home is where we start from: Essays by a psychoanalyst.* New York, NY: W. W. Norton & Company, Inc.

4

The Epic Myths
About Your Body
That Keep You
Stuck (and How to
Give Them Up)

I am dreading this evening. I left work and got on the Metro after a long day of retail sales. I was headed to the apartment I shared with roommates and knew my best friend from high school, who arrived earlier in the day, would be waiting for me. We had planned a night out at a club to celebrate the last evening of 1988.At 19, I had already dropped of college and moved to Washington, D.C., on a whim. I worked a minimum wage job with no idea of what a future might look like, much less how to make it happen. My relationships with food and body were nonexistent and I discovered that drugs and alcohol could numb me and take away any feelings in or for my body which was useful after bingeing or long periods of restriction. This non-embodied and destructive state made me a more interesting person as was evidenced, to my way of thinking, by the colorful group of friends with whom I now spent most of my time and the adventures I collected during episodes of risky behavior. I found it amusing, not realizing that I put myself in life-threatening situations time and again.

Most days, despite my best effort, my body issues had enough time to surface before I could numb out. This day had been especially trying as my best friend, Becky, could be extremely critical about her and everyone else's body. I anticipated, as I made my way home, she would likely be dressed in a fabulous new ensemble and I knew the insecurities and inferiority that Becky evoked from me were already dictating my mood. My anxiety increased steadily as the Metro glided toward my stop. I arrived home to a pre-club party in full swing. My roommates and friends were dressed up and enjoying cocktails. I was immediately thankful I did not eat all day. My body felt lighter than it would have if well nourished.

"Get over here, Miss Chev. I'm pouring drinks," demanded my roommate, Robbie, as he poured me a tequila shot. Robbie had a distinct southern Virginia drawl that made his natural proclivity to snark about everyone and everything around him charming despite his intent to deliver what was usually an unkind message.

"You need a couple of shots right away, Chevbu, so you can catch up to us." Chevbu or Bubu were the nicknames Becky had assigned me several years ago after watching a show about Shamu the killer whale. She always used them with a baby like voice that meant to endear me to her, but I was not fooled. I knew from others the epithets were an inside joke meant to comment on my body. I smiled, did three successive shots and followed with a rum and coke chaser. Now I was perfectly numb for the work ahead: finding the perfect combination of fabric and stitching that would push, smash, and command my outer softness inward.
I needed the clothes to transform me so I could be desired and admired. I could only cloak the soft rolls and intersecting curves so much, but if the mirror offered me just a hint of a thinner silhouette tonight I would allow the light and airy party girl part of me to emerge. I changed clothes at least five times that evening and paired each new ensemble with a tequila shot coupled with the never-empty glass of some other type of spirit. After more than an hour of preparation, I finally walked in to the living room to mingle with friends and prepare to leave for the club. As we began walking out the door, I felt the room begin to spin and the voices around me sounded further and further away.

"Try to catch her or she will hit her head," someone said.

I did not make it to the club that New Year's Eve. In fact, I do not remember a thing after I began to fall backwards.

The next morning, I woke to the sound of voices hovering over me. Very slowly, the voices got louder and I began to sense light. After some time, I opened my eyes and realized I was on my bed and two women were looking at me and laughing.

"Are you okay?" asked Becky.

"We thought you were going to die," said Cathy, a roommate.

"Why?" I asked.

Cathy began to laugh. "Because you vomited all over the walls of the living room and hallway, then passed out. I stayed with you and didn't go to the club because I thought you might have alcohol poisoning."

"You were a mess last night BuBu. You missed a great time at the club," Becky said as she encouraged me to get up and join her for what would become a binge session; something we often did together after a night of drinking.

▶ BODY HATRED

The urge to diet is rooted in oppression.

—Rachel Cole

How much did Florence Nightingale weigh when she founded modern nursing? How much did Rosa Parks weigh when she took a seat on that bus? How much did Malala Yousafzai weigh when she started writing about the lives of girls in Pakistan living under Taliban rule? You don't know? That's the right answer! *Because it doesn't matter.*

—Martha Beck

Body hate, despite being the norm, is not *normal*. We are not born to judge our body, nor do we develop body hatred naturally. It is learned. The degree to which our self-worth is connected to body acceptance is acquired from both family and cultural narratives. Especially for women, body shape and size are synonymous with social status and personal worth. Liking or disliking something about your appearance is far more important to psychological well-being than it should be. How you look is not about aesthetic preferences, but about your social acceptability. For people with BED, internal negative judgment of their bodies feels reasonable and true.

I recently addressed an audience of several hundred people (almost all women) at, ironically, a self-compassion summit. I asked the audience members to raise their hands if they saw their body as acceptable, right now, as it is. Ten women, out of hundreds, very tentatively raised their hands. This is impact of the cultural milieu in which your relationship with food and your body develops. In such a place, you barely stand a chance to see your body as your home, with the compassion and gentleness it actually deserves.

Most of us with BED learned to dislike our bodies early on. I recall my first diet at the young age of 10, and I am definitely not an exception in this regard. In a study of children aged 9–14, approximately *half* of the girls responded they were already unhappy with their size (Dion et al., 2016). Given the ubiquitousness of the message, this early adaptation of the thin ideal is no surprise. The average American woman is 5'4" tall and weighs 140 pounds. The average American model is 5'11" tall and weighs 117 pounds. The average fashion model is thinner than 98 percent of American women (Smolak, Striegel-Moore, & Levine, 1996).

▶ THE POWER OF STIGMA

Certain traits elevate our social status: young, white, wealthy, and heterosexual top the list. But perhaps the one still most accepted is being thin. The thin ideal impacts most everyone, regardless of their actual body size. Research tells us over and over that these body shaming experiences, shared and witnessed by so many of us, are *causal* factors in the development of binge eating disorder. Despite their danger, the messages persist.

Weight stigma, perhaps the most insidious force in the development of BED, is discrimination or prejudice based on weight, size, or shape. In fact, in studies in the United States, weight-based discrimination has been demonstrated to have similar prevalence to race-based discrimination, with fatter and younger people being subjected to the highest levels of weight-based discrimination. Weight stigma significantly impacts how people of various sizes are treated in our culture and it is used to justify overt and covert forms of discrimination (Puhl, Andreyeva, & Brownell, 2008). Common weight-based stereotypes assume people in larger bodies are lazy, lack self-discipline, have poor willpower, are less intelligent, or lack character. Media portrayals of people with larger body sizes create and reinforce biased attitudes. Consider the degree to which weight gain and loss is a focus for celebrities and public figures. We use the word "fat" as an insult, not simply a descriptor. Women in the public eye are scrutinized for the slightest changes in shape and appearance. Oprah's weight changes have been in the headlines for years, both gains and losses.

Weight stigma packs a life-altering punch. According to Rebecca Puhl of the Yale Rudd Center for Food Policy and Obesity:

> Research spanning several decades has documented consistent weight bias and stigmatization in employment, health care, schools, the media, and interpersonal relationships. For overweight and obese youth, weight stigmatization translates into pervasive victimization, teasing, and bullying. Multiple adverse outcomes are associated with exposure to weight stigmatization, including depression, anxiety, low self-esteem, body dissatisfaction, suicidal ideation, poor academic performance, lower physical activity, maladaptive eating behaviors, and avoidance of health care.

Weight stigma can be overt or subtle, directed or unintended, and profoundly damaging to self-worth. Intentional or unintentional verbal, behavioral, or environmental indignities that communicate hostility or negativity—called micro-aggressions—toward people who do not meet the thin ideal are common. Suggesting weight loss to a patient who did not bring weight as a concern to their doctor's appointment is an all too common example. Weight loss or appearance-related compliments are also examples of micro-aggressions. They assume thin is necessarily a person's goal and that the weight loss is *necessarily* an improvement. Sectioning larger clothes in the back of stores (if they are available at all), or charging more for airplane seats are also common examples.

Weight stigma weaves the threat of weight-related judgment into the cultural milieu. While it is more damaging to *be* bigger than to *be afraid of* being bigger, stigma affects everyone regardless of size. "If you're in a body and you live in a Westernized culture, you're impacted by weight stigma," my colleague Deb Burgard once said. Even being thin does not render you safe from body shame.

▶ BLAME AND SHAME

Our culture tells us to place blame directly on people in larger bodies for failing to meet the thin ideal, as though blame were both justifiable and perhaps even *necessary* to motivate adopting healthier lifestyle behaviors. This is based on the presumption that being larger is *intrinsically* unhealthy and pathological, and necessarily the result of lifestyle choices. Society regularly regards bigger people as unhealthy, and their behaviors as the direct cause for their size or shape. People in a larger body must be lazy and must overeat. Such cultural assumptions provide the foundation for weight stigma. Not only is this stigma viewed as a beneficial incentive for weight loss, but it is also assumed that the "condition of obesity" is under personal control, and that weight loss *necessarily* means improved health. The social influence of weight shaming and blaming is considered justified to produce the culturally sanctioned change. For many with BED, this fits into their preexisting expectations of the world around them, and their own shaming internal narratives.

What we know from clinical experience is this: shame is not a useful vehicle for long-term change (assuming change is a reasonable or viable goal in a given circumstance). Weight stigma is no different. In fact, shame and stigmatizing experiences *cause* binge eating. Among both clinical and nonclinical samples of higher-weight adults, weight stigma has been documented as a significant risk factor for depression, low self-esteem, and body dissatisfaction (Puhl & Heuer, 2010). These findings persist despite control for variables including age, gender, onset of weight increase, and BMI. Rather than being associated with excess body weight in itself, negative psychological outcomes are linked with experiences of weight-based *stigmatization*. A recent study examining a nationally representative sample of more than 9,000 obese adults found that perceived weight discrimination was significantly associated with a current diagnosis of mood and anxiety disorders and mental health services use, even after control for sociodemographic characteristics and perceived stress (Simon et al., 2007). If weight stigma promoted healthier lifestyle behaviors and weight loss, then the past several decades of fat shaming and blaming should be accompanied by a significant reduction in overall BMI of the population. This is not the case; in fact, BMI continues to *climb*. A recent study found weight discrimination has even increased by 66 percent over the past 10 years, even after control for a range of variables including BMI (Puhl & Heuer, 2010). Not only are there more higher-weight people, but there are also more people reporting discrimination on the basis of their weight. From this outcome, one might ask if it is the stigmatization that is problematic.

Our obsession with thinness and rampant efforts at dieting appear not to have solved the alleged "obesity epidemic." It might be more logically defensible to look for other causes, but instead the culturally sanctioned obsession with thinness blames the victim for not meeting the ideal of thin. In fact, the reality is this: dieting *causes* the body to activate its natural reaction to behavioral weight loss efforts with *weight restoration.* (This will be discussed more in the next chapter). Additionally, a number of studies have consistently demonstrated weight stigma increases the likelihood of engaging in unhealthy eating behaviors and lower levels of physical activity, both of which can exacerbate weight gain and enhance the cycle of binge eating (Puhl & Heuer, 2010). Several studies have demonstrated higher-weight children who experience weight-based teasing are more likely to engage in binge eating and unhealthy weight control behaviors compared with higher-weight peers who are not teased (Eisenberg & Neumark-Sztainer, 2008). Weight-based teasing in youths predicts binge eating and extreme weight control practices 5 years later (Neumark-Sztainer et al., 2006). Weight-based victimization of overweight youths has been linked to lower levels of physical activity, negative attitudes about sports, and lower participation in physical activity. These symptoms also speak to the potentially traumatic impact of weight-related bullying and teasing, further reinforcing the drive to go to food to soothe the fear and shame that accompany the experience of rejection.

Similar findings have emerged for adults. In both clinical and nonclinical samples, adults who experience weight-based stigmatization engage in more frequent binge eating, are at increased risk for maladaptive eating patterns and eating disorder symptoms, and are more likely to have a diagnosis of binge eating disorder. Some research has found that experiences of stigma increase vulnerability to poor psychological functioning, which in turn increases risk for binge eating behaviors (Puhl & Brownell, 2006).

In another a study of more than 2,400 women in the "overweight" and "obese" categories (based on BMI) who belonged to a weight loss support organization, 79 percent reported coping with weight stigma on multiple occasions by eating more food, and 75 percent reported coping by refusing to diet (Tsai & Wadden, 2005). Similar research demonstrated that "overweight" and "obese" women (based on BMI) who internalized negative weight stigma reported more frequent binge eating and refusal to diet compared with adults in the same BMI categories who did not internalize stigma. Research shows adults who experience weight stigma are also more likely to avoid exercise. While refusing to diet may, in fact, be a healthful choice, in this situation it is probably not motivated by self-care, but rather by hopelessness and shame (Puhl & Heuer, 2010).

Simply going to the doctor often induces significant anxiety and shame. For many of my clients (among those who have access to medical care), the threat of being weighed or being shamed for their size keeps them from seeking needed services. Research shows health care professionals are a significant source of weight-based prejudice (Tylka et al., 2014). Stigmatizing attitudes have been demonstrated by nurses and medical students, psychologists, dietitians, and fitness professionals. In her research, Rebecca Puhl of the Yale Rudd Center for Food Policy and Obesity finds that patients may well believe that such shaming remarks are warranted, deserved, and appropriate. To compound the problem, many health care providers believe patients are to blame for avoiding the doctor in the first place (Puhl & Heuer, 2009).

Weight-related bullying for kids is even more distressing. In a recent national survey of "overweight" sixth graders (as defined by BMI), 24 percent of the boys and 30 percent of the girls experienced *daily* teasing, bullying, or rejection because of their size. The number doubles for high school students, with 58 percent of boys and 63 percent of girls experiencing weight-based teasing. Unless bullying is addressed by caregivers who can help a child or adolescent and challenge the negative messages about their weight, these experiences often result in the toxic shame of complex trauma. In fact, when asked about the impact of weight-based bullying, 70 percent found such experiences to be pivotal in the development of their eating disorder (Lumeng et al., 2010).

▶ THIN PRIVILEGE

Most people with BED have been many sizes over time. In my adult life I have been a size 10 and a size 26, and everything in between. The world was indeed a very different place at each end of the size spectrum. The attention and respect afforded me as a 10 was definitely denied as a 26. I was often overlooked when my body was bigger; I disappeared as my weight increased. At a size 10, I was frequently congratulated for working so hard; at a 26 people assumed I had given up.

Not surprisingly then, discrimination based on weight and shape is common. In one study, the data suggested strong evidence of employment bias against people in higher-weight bodies (Puhl & Brownell, 2001). The applicant's body weight explained about 35 percent of the variance in the hiring decision and was the most powerful predictor of employment in this experiment. Higher-weight women experience greater employment discrimination than higher-weight men. Job applicants in larger bodies were no more likely to be hired for a position requiring minimal public contact than they were for a job requiring extensive public contact. This speaks to an internalized weight bias more than any perceived difference in ability to perform a specific job (Pingitore et al., 1994).

The privilege afforded to thin people shows itself in many ways, well beyond the job market. Thin people are assumed to be fit and healthy; larger people are assumed to be in some measure of ill health. Doctors may suspect weight-related diabetes, high blood pressure, high cholesterol, or other diagnoses before even considering metabolic imbalances, genetics, or other natural explanations. Many insurance companies deny surgeries such as knee or hip replacement until weight is lost, even when the pain may stop the person from exercise and movement. Insurance companies may charge higher premiums based solely on weight without considering other health indices. Bigger is presumed to be pathological, even though there is insufficient evidence to support this hypothesis. In fact, the *Journal of the American Medical Association* published a study (Flegal et al., 2013) that reviewed data from nearly a hundred large epidemiological studies to determine the relationship between body mass and mortality risks and found all adults categorized as "overweight" and most of those categorized as "obese" have a *lower* mortality risk than those considered of "normal" weight. Human bodies can be—and are—healthy at many different sizes.

Additionally, thin people are not typically assumed to be a "work in progress." I hear over and over about the strangers that find it acceptable to comment to my clients in higher-weight bodies about their eating behaviors, food choices, and weight. For example, people feel obliged to comment on the food in my clients' grocery carts in the name of trying to be helpful. Family and friends suggest weight loss programs unprompted, simply assuming weight loss to be a goal. A fat body is treated as a an ongoing project to be completed when the person finds an intervention they can "stick with." Thin people can eat whatever they wish in public with much less judgment, intervention, or ridicule. They are not considered lazy or unprofessional. "You have such a pretty face"—a comment my clients and I have heard many times—implies your beauty goes to *waste* in a bigger body. There is often a qualifier when people describe larger friends: "She's bigger, but really nice/smart/funny." Consumer choices for clothing clearly reflect thin privilege. Plus-sized clothing is often more expensive, of lesser quality, and poorer design. Fashion designs for larger sizes are meant to hide figure "flaws." Rarely do we see large people model clothing (above a size 12 or 14), and when we do, the products are intended *only* for large people. While this is changing some in the last few years (a bigger range of sizes has been added to some popular labels and stores), the change has been met with derision and ridicule from many corners.

▶ WHAT ABOUT WEIGHT AND HEALTH?

According to the dominant cultural narrative, a BMI above "normal" is unhealthy and therefore, people should do something about it. In fact, the relationship between weight and health is nuanced, complex, and to a great degree, still not understood. The truth is, for any given individual, *we cannot assume thinner means healthier*.

Weight became a focus of consciousness in the United States around the turn of the 20th century. "I would sooner die than be fat," declared Amelia Summerville, author of the 1916 volume *Why Be Fat? Rules for Weight-Reduction and the Preservation of Youth and Health*. Weight loss drugs hit the mainstream marketplace in the 1920s, when doctors began prescribing thyroid medications for weight control. In the 1930s, 2,4-dinitrophenol came along, followed by amphetamines, diuretics, laxatives, and diet pills like fen-phen, all of which caused side effects ranging from troublesome to fatal. Next, the use of height and weight charts such as body mass index (BMI) by insurance companies introduced people and their physicians to a standardized notion of what they *should* weigh. Weight became a clinical issue, using new words like *adipose, overweight,* and *obese* to describe body size and to render medical opinions. The word *overweight* implies you're over the "correct" weight. The word *obese,* from the Latin *obesus,* or "eaten until fat," conveys both clinical assessment and moral judgment.

This attitude inspired a number of new and horrifying treatments including jaw-wiring and brain surgeries that burned lesions into the hypothalamus. Bariatric surgery is the latest of these attempts to circumvent the body. In 2000, according to the Centers for Disease Control, about 37,000 bariatric surgeries were performed in the United States; by 2013, the number had risen to 220,000. The best estimates suggest about half of those who have surgery regain some or all of the weight they lose. While such surgeries are safer now than they were 10 years ago, they still lead to complications for many, including long-term malnutrition, intestinal blockages, disordered eating, and death. These surgeries are not cures for BED either; binge eating is still possible following bariatric surgery, and can be much more danger-ous (Chao et al., 2017).

The prevalence of these treatments would suggest the connections between weight, nutrition, and health have been established through scientific and medical research. Indeed the opposite is the case. We simply do not know at this time what makes for a healthy diet. Nor do we know if everyone should eat the same things in the same proportions, or get the same amount of exercise for optimal health. In addition, much of the research is predicated on faith that when fat people lose weight, they become healthier. The evi-dence says otherwise. In fact, it suggests that even if you lose weight, *you will always need fewer calories and need to exercise more or the weight will very likely return.* Our bodies seem determined to return and remain at the higher weight. Thus, obesity treatments offer a solution to something that may not be a problem, and a solution that does not even work as promised (Bacon, 2010).

Right now, based on statistics from the Center for Disease Control, we know weight is *linked* with certain diseases, most strongly Type 2 diabetes. But correlation does not equal causation. Weight gain may be an early *symptom* of Type 2 diabetes instead of the *cause* for some people. There are thin dia-betics and fat people with stable blood sugar. Perhaps a third factor causes both weight gain and diabetes. People who lose weight often see their blood sugar improve, but that may be an effect of calorie reduction rather than weight loss. Type 2 diabetics who have bariatric surgery may go into complete remission after only seven days, long before they lose much weight, because they're eating only a few hundred calories per day. This is not sustainable, even frequently for those who have had bariatric interventions.

Additionally, disease is often related to specific dietary choices. For instance, eating fast food once a week has been linked to high blood pressure in teens (Pereira et al., 2005). And eating fruits and vegetables every day is associated with lower risk of heart disease. But science has yet to establish causality. Higher BMIs have been linked to a higher risk of developing Type 2 diabetes, heart disease, and certain cancers, especially esophageal, pancreatic, and breast cancers. But weight loss is not necessarily linked to lower levels of these diseases. A 2004 study suggested patients with Type 2 diabetes who *maintained their weight* had the best prognosis (Field et al., 2004). The only study to follow subjects for more than 5 years, the 2013 Look AHEAD study, found no significant difference between people with Type 2 diabetes who lost weight as those who didn't for heart attacks, strokes, and death (The Look AHEAD Research Group, 2013). Additionally, study after study has turned up what has come to be known as the "obesity paradox": higher-weight patients with heart disease, heart failure, diabetes, kidney disease, pneumonia, and many other chronic diseases fare better and live longer than those of "normal" weight (Pi-Sunyer, 2014).

We clearly don't fully understand the relationship between weight and overall mortality. It is almost universally assumed the higher your BMI, the higher your risk for early death. But Katherine Flegal, an epidemiologist with the CDC, consistently found the highest death rates among those at *either* end of the BMI spectrum and the *lowest* rates in the "overweight" and "mildly obese" categories (Flegal et al., 2013). Study after study turns up this alleged paradox; "obese" patients with disease live longer than those of "normal" weight with disease.

Why do doctors keep prescribing treatments that don't work for a condition that may be benign? For one thing, our cultural narrative encourages thin people to remain invested in their own privilege. Additionally, there is a great deal of money at stake in "treating obesity." With the medicalization of weight, doctors who discuss weight with their patients will be able to add that diagnosis code to their bill, often then charging more for the visit.

An entire industry is predicated on this paradigm. For example, in 2013, the *New England Journal of Medicine* published "Myths, Presumptions, and Facts About Obesity." The authors (Casazza et al., 2013) dismissed the often-observed link between weight cycling and mortality, saying it was "probably due to confounding by health status"—code for "we just can't believe this could be true"—and went on to plug meal replacements like Jenny Craig, medications, and bariatric surgery. Five of the 20 authors disclosed financial support from sponsors in weight-loss-related industries.

▶ DIETING FAILS TO PROVIDE REDEMPTION

At all costs, including risks to our health, we are told to avoid being fat. Weight concern endures through life, and starts early. Forty to 60 percent of elementary school girls (ages 6–12) are concerned about their weight or about becoming too fat (Cash & Smolak, 2012). More than 50 percent of teen girls and 30 percent of teen boys use unhealthy weight control behaviors such as skipping meals, fasting, smoking cigarettes, vomiting, and taking laxatives (Story et al., 1991). In another more recent study, over half of the females between ages 18 and 25 would prefer to be run over by a truck than to be fat, and two-thirds would choose to be mean or stupid rather than fat (Gaesser, 2002). Despite these powerfully entrenched messages, findings clearly indicate dieting and unhealthy weight control behaviors, as reported by adolescents, actually *predict* significant weight gain over time. In fact, adolescent girls who diet frequently are far more likely to binge eat as girls who don't (Neumark-Sztainer et al., 2007).

According to a recent study (Slof-Op't Landt et al., 2017), dieting was reported by 50 to 60 percent of 35- to 65-year-old women and about 30 percent of 45- to 65-year-old men. Fear of weight gain was most prevalent in women between 16 and 25 (73.2 to 74.3 percent), and in 25- to 55-year-old men (43.2 to 46.1 percent). In another study, a high percentage of college females considered themselves "overweight" or "obese," despite having a BMI in the "normal" category. Dieting was practiced by 43 percent, and 32 percent were avoiding weight gain, despite 78 percent having a "healthy" BMI (Fayet et al., 2012). With so many often-doomed attempts to lose weight, it is no wonder that, according to Marketdata Enterprises, Americans spent more than $64 billion in 2016 to try to lose weight.

Research tells us 95 percent of all dieters will regain lost weight in 1 to 5 years, while 35 percent will progress to pathological dieting. Dieters may well lose weight in the short term (thus suggesting some efficacy of dieting), but the chance of keeping if off for 5 years or more is the same as the chance of surviving metastatic lung cancer: about 5 percent (Brown, 2015). While many studies demonstrate weight loss from dieting in the short-term, such studies have significant problems including small sample sizes, underrepresentation of men, limited generalizability, a lack of blinded ascertainment of the outcome, a lack of data on adherence to assigned diets, and a large loss in follow-up participation (Simons-Morton, Obarzanek, & Cutler, 2006). Additionally, most weight loss trials do not have long-term follow-up; thus, the results over the subsequent 2 to 5 years, when weight gain is most likely to occur, often go unreported (Robison & Carrier, 2004).There is basically no good news here. Dieting offers no redemption from the shame and fear of social rejection that comes from being fat. Indeed, the "cure" seems to be making the patients sick.

▶ USURPING OUR POWER AND OUR BODIES

"A culture fixated on female thinness is not an obsession about female beauty, but an obsession about female obedience. Dieting is the most potent political sedative in women's history; a quietly mad population is a tractable one," wrote Naomi Wolf (1990). Unfortunately, little has changed since this was written. Under what has long been called the tyranny of slenderness, women are forbidden to become large; they must take up as little space as possible. The very contours of a woman's body—fuller breasts and rounded hips—become signs of being "overweight" instead of sexual maturity. The body ideal is the physique of early adolescence, narrow and immature, a body with limited substance or power. The expectation of hairless skin continues the narrative of youth, as does the celebration of a face that never shows lines of experience or depth of thought. "The face of the ideally feminine woman must never display the marks of character, wisdom, and experience that we so admire in men," noted Sandra Lee Bartky (1990). Women are expected to look inexperienced, virginal, and powerless. If they do not, they should at least be seen in constant pursuit of such goals. Thus, fat people are considered more tolerable, and seen as more sympathetic, if they are trying to "fix" their alleged problem.

> "Since I was as young as I can remember, the home environment included statements directed at me and my sister from adults, my

father in particular, like, 'TYTI!' which meant tuck your tummy in," a client recalled. I remember hearing "a moment on the lips, a lifetime on the hips."

Imagine a woman at home in her body, as is, cherishing her health instead of trying to fix something perceived to be broken. It would be an act of revolution. Of course, it's not only weight that impacts body image.

> I've always had short hair. The messages from society I get about this have impacted me a lot. What does it mean to have short hair? Can I be feminine with short hair? Is short hair a symbol or synonymous for lesbian or butch or something else? Is short hair attractive? Don't most guys want the long luscious locks?

> I have very dark skin, not the light brown considered acceptable. Somehow, my body should be not only thin, but less black. I can't seem to do either.

> I am often told how well I look for my age. I hear it more frequently than anything about the five books I've written.

Body hate happens principally as a result of wanting to be accepted by very judgmental systems; it is not about objective truth. Looking a certain way may be an aesthetic preference, but it should not be reason enough for body shame or disgust. There is no inherent reason not to feel compassion and protection for one's body. Yet, almost no women in our culture feel this way. Our internalization of the cultural messaging makes a handful of companies and commercial interests a lot of money. Shame sells, and we're buying. "The patriarchy has taught you to edit everything that you put in your mouth, as well as everything that comes out of it," notes Desiree Lynn Adaway, coach and consultant to organizations building resilient, equitable, and inclusive work environments. In support of recovery from BED, and because it's the right thing to do for those who come after us, our buying into the shame and blame story needs to stop.

▶ BODY AS HOME

Making peace with our bodies is integral to recovery from BED. When body shame narratives remain unchallenged, they drive the desire to go to food to soothe, rebel, or escape. But, how do you dispute these messages when they are so long-standing and ubiquitous? How do you begin to allow something different? Recovering in a culture where obsession with thinness and dieting is the norm is definitely not easy. It requires spotting something in society that has been internalized into the mantras of your inner critic parts. And how do you deal with the grief about the time you've lost in pursuing a shame-based, mostly societally constructed, goal of weight loss? Working toward being thin holds so much hope for many people with BED; it is the end goal that will make everything else OK. As with much of recovery, change comes from self-compassion, allowing your story and all your feelings, honoring your own body, and, as you are able, advocating for change in the larger world.

Many of my clients ask me how they could possibly love their bodies without "fixing" them in some significant way. How is it possible to see beauty in something so long maligned? The body positivity movement has encouraged us to accept and embrace our flaws. These messages are certainly well-intentioned, and may feel supportive and inspiring for many women. I would suggest, however, this keeps the focus of our body's worth primarily on its appearance. I see the most sustained recovery in my clinical work when clients are able to shift this whole paradigm, from body as billboard to body as home. Our appearance can be a creative expression, but body as home suggests our body's primary role is to be the place where we live and flourish, strive to feel safe and protected, and experience our surroundings. It is deserving of the best care and sustenance, regardless of physical appearance. In fact, I believe we would do well to significantly expand our definitions of beauty:

> It doesn't make sense to call ourselves ugly, because we don't really see ourselves. We don't watch ourselves sleeping in bed, curled up and silent with chests rising and falling with our own rhythm. We don't see ourselves reading a book, eyes fluttering and glowing. You don't see yourself looking at someone with love and care inside your heart. There's no mirror in your way when you're laughing and smiling and happiness is leaking out of you. You would know exactly how bright and beautiful you are if you saw yourself in the moments where you are truly your authentic self.
>
> —Unknown

The self-compassion this quote encourages plays a pivotal role in all of recovery. Self-compassion is predicated on knowing you are worth being cared for and protected, *right now, as is.* It is the most basic tool for healing. In the context of body image, self-compassion is fundamentally about honoring our bodies for their *work*, for being our homes, day in and day out, as best they are able. It is about being able to see beauty in yourself and others, and also being ok with seeing the ugly, the messy, the utter imperfection of who you are. Is it a joy to play with beauty? Fashion? For some people, yes it is. Might you still feel a longing to look a certain way? Of course! These are very old messages, and your eyes have been trained from a very early age to look for beauty in particular ways. But you can come to meet these feelings with compassion. You can come to know the desire to look a certain way is often muddled with the fear of not being lovable. You can come to reach out to yourself with reassurance and tenderness for all the pain you have endured at the hands of these narratives. Recovery is not about never longing to be thin, or to look a certain way. It is about how you deal with these thoughts and feelings when they emerge, meeting them not as truth, but as a symptom of a damaging, and lucrative, system of oppression.

▶ A CHANGE IN FOCUS

Imagine that your current body—the one you are in *right this minute*— was considered absolutely acceptable. Really allow this idea for a moment or two. Suppose its shape, size, texture, color, gender (if you define it), are exactly as they "should" be. Did anything in your body change as you considered? Any sensations or emotions you noticed? It is very likely that the world, both inside and out, would feel immediately, significantly, different. What in your life might change? How would your behavior, relationships, dreams, or focus change? Would your clothing change? How would the way you care for your body differ? What might it be like to see your body as a functional masterpiece, even though imperfect? What might allow you to see bodies, first and foremost, as homes for ourselves and all the people we love?

Deb Burgard, Ph.D., and others have developed a powerful model that can help us find the way back home to a better relationship with our bodies, as they are, right now. This model, called Health at Every Size (HAES®), invites us to shift our perspective on our bodies from weight-based to well-being. This means, on the individual level, that your primary job with regard to your body is to listen to it, and meet its needs as best you are able. As we have seen, a focus on weight, regardless of our actual size, leaves us feeling powerless and objectified, shameful, and afraid of rejection. A focus on well-being, however, allows us to feel powerful, cherished and protected.

The basic tenets for Health at Every Size are as follows:

▶ Focus on the quality of your day-to-day life experience

▶ Honor your varying needs for food and movement as you are able

▶ Find sustainable, adaptive ways to take care of yourself that allow for imperfection and change

▶ Accept your body knows best about weight; when you are taking care of yourself, your body will find its sustainable natural weight

While these tenets ought to be intuitive and easy to follow, they are typically anything but. It may be intuitive to apply a HAES® philosophy to *other* people, but using this wisdom to treat yourself will probably feel quite revolutionary. Trust your body. It is your home, and *its value does not change if it gets larger or smaller, if it ages, or when it becomes ill.*

The HAES® model rejects the use of weight, size, or BMI as a primary indicator of health or need for treatment. It also rejects the myth that weight is simply a result of personal choices. Unlike dieting, HAES® does not consider pursuing health as a moral imperative or individual obligation. Health status should never be used to judge, oppress, or determine the value of an individual. Indeed, there are many sociocultural and psychological roadblocks to accessing resources that support body care. A HAES® model invites us on both an individual and cultural level to challenge systems that perpetuate shame and a lack of access to the tools that support well-being.

▶ MAKING THE CHANGES: SOME FIRST STEPS

Over the years, my clients and I have found a number of practices and reminders helpful in healing body shame using POWR and adopting a

HAES® approach. When you hear body shaming messages, using POWR may look something like this:

▶ Pause and center into Self energy with square breathing.

▶ Open and allow the thoughts and feelings of these body messages to come to your attention. Simply notice them. Are they associated with any particular part (child, teenager, etc.)?

▶ Wisely consider these messages. Are they distorted or damaging? What triggered them? Why are they here now? What is the fear behind them? Was body shame triggered because of another underlying fear or shame? Or, were they triggered by something in the environment (i.e., gowns too small at the doctor's office, a magazine article extolling the latest weight loss tips)?

▶ Respond with care. What do you really need right now? Do you need reassurance? Do you need to advocate with someone for your body's needs or protection? Do you need to stop what you're doing right now (is it a shaming activity, like changing clothes multiple times or weighing yourself)?

Using the POWR process with body shame is predicated on challenging many of the messages we have internalized from family and culture. To build the POWR muscle around body image, consider the following:

▶ Learn your own mythology of weight loss. Everyone's messages are slightly different, and vary in tone and frequency. Ask yourself: What do I believe will change when I lose weight? What would I allow myself to do that I don't do now? Consider doing those things anyway.

▶ Allow feeling loss and fear when challenging the idealization of thin. It will feel wrong and scary to do so; it will not stay that way. Remember, you are not settling for something, or giving up on how you look. You are recovering from the cult of body shame and weight stigma. Expect to feel rejection and resistance to change. You are creating space for your body to get the best care possible no matter what, and freeing yourself from many of the bonds that reinforce binge eating.

▶ Grieve lost time, energy, and money trying to lose weight. I have had clients chose a ritual—like a burial or goodbye ceremony—for dieting. As with all forms of grief, these feelings will come and go.

▶ Think about all the things your body can do. It is amazing! Consider all the experiences your body has survived. Notice its power and strength. Notice scars and stretch marks and wrinkles; they are all evidence of the story of your life.

▶ If looking in the mirror at any given time is causing you to judge harshly, *stop looking immediately* and use POWR. You are being hijacked by old narratives and will not see your body accurately or compassionately.

▶ What is your heart's definition of "beauty"? Are the people most beautiful to you necessarily attractive (according to cultural standards) physically? Does it even matter? Is beauty more important to you than you would like it to be?

▶ Do something kind for your body—a massage, wear a soft tee shirt, use lotion, wear perfume, stretch your muscles. See what happens in your attitude toward your body as a result.

▶ Watch for your judgments of others' weight and appearance. Such judgments damage you, too. Offer forgiveness to yourself when you judge, and compassion toward others.

▶ Consider how you feel about someone you love whose body is imperfect. How would you talk to them about their harsh self-judgments? Allow yourself the same voice.

▶ Censor outside messages to the degree you are able. If something makes you feel badly about your body, avoid it (magazines, social media, certain gyms or workout classes, etc.).

▶ Stop weighing yourself. There is nothing to learn from the scale that your body does not know already. If this feels too scary, try stopping for one week. Use the POWR process when the urge to weigh arises.

▶ Freaked out by seeing a reflection or photograph? Remember, you are not one static moment in time. You are dynamic, moving, living. Your beauty is in inhabiting your space and being you, not what is caught in one frozen moment.

▶ If you enjoy doing so, dress to honor who you are. Allow appearance to be about creative expression when you desire to do so. If you love it, wear it.

▶ Get rid of what does not fit. We need to open the closet door and be able to wear everything we see. Your current body defines what the right size is right now.

▶ Physical beauty (as culturally defined) is not a requirement to have the right to be sexual as a woman. If you struggle with feeling sexual desire, there are important fears at play. POWR can help with these messages too, as will the support of therapy to safely explore healing your sexual self. Reclaim sexuality and sensuality on your own terms. What arouses your senses? What messages or experiences inhibit your sexual or sensual self? Decisions about sexuality need to be made not from fear and shame but from gentle compassion, connection, and safety. Move at your own pace in this work. There is no finish line, only the possibility for healing.

▶ Watch for stigmatizing messages from all of the intersecting communities in your life. There may be many appearance-based expectations surrounding you. Try to give yourself permission to examine them closely, and decide for yourself how to address them. Messages may be about your body's weight, skin color, gender, or physical ability.

▶ If you have access to health care, tell your doctor your wishes about weighing and weight talk. If they won't agree, find another one if at all possible.

▶ You may have many people in your life who don't understand the work you're doing in recovery. Find (or create) a community (some resources are listed below).

▶ Body neutrality is different from body positivity. You need not love everything about your body to give it good care.

▶ Allow different kinds of movement. Think of your body as an instrument, not an ornament. What does it like to do? When? For how long? How does your body tell you it desires to move? To rest?

▶ Living in a higher weight body is not easy in this culture. Try to remember weight bias does not mean there is something wrong with *you*. If you experience weight discrimination, consider taking action to challenge it instead.

▶ Feeling good about your body may be upsetting to some people in your life. What do you need to do to be safe? Can you help people learn more about your journey, if you wish to do so?

▶ Exchange shame for righteous indignation. Feeling badly about our bodies *should not be the norm*. Consider how you might contribute your story to the work of changing the cultural narratives about health and weight.

▶ Offer gratitude to your body for always doing its best.

In the next chapter, we will turn our attention to offering our bodies the best care possible. To that end, we will consider the damage done by dieting, and how dieting itself contributes to BED. We will also come to see that, once we let go of the restriction paradigm, our bodies intuitively know how to ask for what they need.

▶ BIBLIOGRAPHY

Annis, N. M., Cash, T. F., & Hrabosky, J. I. (2004). Body image and psychosocial differences among stable average weight, currently overweight, and formerly overweight women: The role of stigmatizing experiences. *Journal of Body Image*, *1*(2), 155–167. Retrieved from http://doi.org/10.1016/j.bodyim.2003.12.001.

Ashmore, J. A., Friedman, K. E., Reichmann, S. K., & Musante, G. (2008). Weight-based stigmatization, psychological distress, and binge eating behavior among obese treatment-seeking adults. *Journal of Eating Behavior, 9*(2), 203–209. Retrieved from http://doi.org/10.1016/j.eatbeh.2007.09.006.

Bacon, L. (2010). *Health at every size: The surprising truth about your weight.* Dallas, TX: BenBella Books.

Bartky, S. L. (1990). *Femininity and domination: Studies in the phenomenology of oppression.* New York, NY: Routledge.

Beck, M. (2017). *Oprah.* Retrieved from www.oprah.com/inspiration/martha-beck-why-new-years-resolutions-fail.

Bishop, J., Middendorf, R., Babin, T., & Tilson, W. (2005). ASPE research brief: Childhood obesity. *Office of the Assistant Secretary for Planning and Evaluation, US Department of Health & Human Services.* Retrieved from http://aspe.hhs.gov/health/reports/child_obesity/.

Brown, H. (2015). *Body of truth: How science, history and culture drive our obsession with weight—and what we can do about it.* Boston, MA: Da Capo Lifelong Books.

Calogero, R. M., Herbozo, S., & Thompson, J. K. (2009). Complimentary weightism: The potential costs of appearance-related commentary for women's self-objectification. *Psychology of Women Quarterly, 33*(1), 120–132. Retrieved from http://dx.doi.org/10.1111/j.1471-6402.2008.01479.x.

Casazza, K., Fontaine, K. R., Astrup, A., Birdh, L. L., Brown, A. W., Brown, M. M. B., . . . Allison, D. B. (2013). Myths, presumptions, and facts about obesity. *New England Journal of Medicine, 368*(5), 446–454. Retrieved from http://doi.org/10.1056/NEJMsa1208051.

Cash, T. F., & Smolak, L. (Eds.). (2012). *Body image: A handbook of science, practice, and prevention.* New York, NY: The Guilford Press.

Chao, A. M., Wadden, T. A., Faulconbridge, L. F., Sarwer, D. B., Webb, V. L., Shaw, J., . . . Williams, N. N. (2017). Binge eating disorder and the outcome of bariatric surgery in a prospective observational study: Two year results. *Obesity (Silver Spring), 24*(11), 2327–2333. Retrieved from http://doi.org/10.1002/oby.21648.

Cole, R. Retrieved from http://soulworkformoms.com/rachelwcole/.

Collins, M. E. (1991). Body figure perceptions and preferences among preadolescent children. *International Journal of Eating Disorders, 10,* 199–208.

Council on Size and Weight Discrimination, Statistics on weight discrimination. (n.d.) *A waste of talent.* The Council on Size and Weight Discrimination, Mt. Marion, NY. Retrieved from www.cswd.org/statistics-2.

Davis-Coelho, K., Waltz, J., & Davis-Coelho, B. (2000). Awareness and prevention of bias against fat clients in psychotherapy. *Professional Psychology: Research and Practice, 31*(6), 682–684. Retrieved from http://dx.doi.org/10.1037/0735-7028.31.6.682.

Dion, J., Hains, J., Vachon, P., Plouffe, J., Laberge, L., Perron, M., . . . Leone, M. (2016). Correlates of body dissatisfaction in children. *Journal of Pediatrics, 171*, 202–207.

Eisenberg, M., & Neumark-Sztainer, D. (2008). Peer harassment and disordered eating. *International Journal of Adolescent Medicine and Health, 20*(2), 155–164.

Fayet, F., Petocz, P., & Samman, S. (2012). Prevalence and correlates of dieting in college women: A cross sectional study. *International Journal of Women's Health, 4*, 405–411. Retrieved from http://doi.org/10.2147/IJWH.S33920.

Field, A. E., Manson, J. E., Laird, N., Williamson, D. F., Willett, W. C., & Colditz, G. A. (2004). Weight cycling and the risk of developing type 2 diabetes among adult women in the United States. *Obesity Research, 12*(2), 267–274. Retrieved from http://doi.org/10.1038/oby.2004.34.

Flegal, K. M., Kit, B. K, Orpana, H., & Graubard, B. I. (2013). Association of all-cause mortality with overweight and obesity using standard body mass index categories: A systematic review and meta-analysis. *Journal of the American Medical Association, 309*(1), 71–82. Retrieved from http://doi.org/10.1001/jama.2012.113905.

Flint, S. W., Cadek, M., Codreanu, S. C., Ivic, V., Zomer, C., & Gomoiu, A. (2016). Obesity discrimination in the recruitment process: "You're *not* hired!" *Frontiers in Psychology, 7*, 647. Retrieved from http://doi.org/10.3389/fpsychq2016.00647.

Gaesser, G. A. (2002). *Big fat lies: The truth about your weight and your health.* Carlsbad, CA: Gürze Books.

Haines, J., Neumark-Sztainer, D., Eisenberg, M. E., & Hannan, P. J. (2006). Weight teasing and disordered eating behaviors in adolescents: Longitudinal findings from Project EAT (Eating Among Teens). *Pediatrics, 117*(2), e209–e215. Retrieved from http://doi.org/10.1542/peds.2005-1242.

Hatzenbuehler, M. L., Keyes, K. M., & Hasin, D. S. (2009). Associations between perceived weight discrimination and the prevalence of psychiatric disorders in the general population. *Obesity (Silver Spring), 17*(11), 2033–2039. Retrieved from http://doi.org/10.1038/oby.2009.131.

Hudson, J. I., Hiripi, E., Pope, H. G. Jr., & Kessler, R. C. (2007). The prevalence and correlates of eating disorders in the National Comorbidity Survey Replication.

Biological Psychiatry, 61(3), 348–358. Retrieved from http://doi.org/10.1016/j. biopsych.2.

Jackson, T. D., Grilo, C. M., & Masheb, R. M. (2000). Teasing history, onset of obesity, current eating disorder psychopathology, body dissatisfaction, and psychological functioning in binge eating disorder. *Obesity Research, 8*(6). Retrieved from http://doi.org/451-8.10.1038/oby.2000.56.

Kilbourne, J. (1994). Still killing us softly: Advertising and the obsession with thinness. In P. Fallon, M. Katzman, & S. Wooley (Eds.), *Feminist perspectives on eating disorders* (pp. 395–419). New York, NY: The Guilford Press.

Køster-Rasmussen, R., Simonsen, M. K., Siersma, V., Henriksen, J. E., Heitmann, B. L., & de Fine Olivarius, N. (2016). Intentional weight loss and longevity in overweight patients with type 2 diabetes: A population-based cohort study. *Plos One, 11*(1), e0146889. Retrieved from http://doi.org/10.1371/journal.pone.0146889.

Levine, M. P., Piran, N., & Stoddard, C. (1999). Mission more probable: Media literacy, activism, and advocacy as primary prevention. In N. Piran, M. P. Levine, & C. Steiner-Adair (Eds.), *Preventing eating disorders: A handbook of interventions and special challenges* (pp. 1–25). Philadelphia, PA: Brunner/Mazel.

The Look AHEAD Research Group. (2013). Cardiovascular effects of intensive lifestyle intervention in type 2 diabetes. *New England Journal of Medicine, 369*, 145–154. Retrieved from http://doi.org/10.1056/HEJMoa1212914.

Lumeng, J. C., Forrest, P., Appugliese, D. P., Kaciroti, N., Corwyn, R. F., & Bradley, R. H. (2010). Weight status as a predictor of being bullied in third through sixth grades. *Pediatrics, 125*(6), e1301–e1307. Retrieved from http://doi.org/10.1542/peds.2009-0774.

Marketdata LLC. (2017). *The U.S. weight loss & diet control market*. Tampa, FL: Marketdata Enterprises. Retrieved from www.webwire.com/ViewPressRel. asp?aId=209054.

Mellin, L., McNutt, S., Hu, Y., Schreiber, G. B., Crawford, P., & Obarzanek, E. (1991). A longitudinal study of the dietary practices of black and white girls 9 and 10 years old at enrollment: The NHLBI growth and health study. *Journal of Adolescent Health, 10*, 23–37.

Musolino, C., Warin, M., Wade, T., & Gilchrist, P. (2016). Developing shared understandings of recovery and care: A qualitative study of women with eating disorders who resist therapeutic care. *Journal of Eating Disorders, 4*, 36. Retrieved from http://doi.org/10.1186/s40337-016-0114-2.

Myers, A., & Rosen, J. C. (1999). Obesity stigmatization and coping: Relation to mental health symptoms, body image, and self-esteem. *International*

Journal of Obesity, 23(3), 221–230. Retrieved from www.ncbi.nlm.nih.gov/pubmed/10193866.

Neumark-Sztainer, D., Wall, M., Guo, J., Story, M., Haines, J., & Eisenberg, M. (2006). Obesity, disordered eating, and eating disorders in a longitudinal study of adolescents: How do dieters fare five years later? *Journal of the American Dietetic Association, 106*(4), 559–568. Retrieved from http://doi.org/10.1016/j.jada.2006.01.003.

Neumark-Sztainer, D., Wall, M., Haines, J., Story, M., & Eisenberg, M. E. (2007). Why does dieting predict weight gain in adolescents? Findings from project EAT-II: A 5-year longitudinal study. *Journal of the American Dietetic Association, 107*(3), 448–455. Retrieved from http://doi.org/10.1016/j.jada.2006.12.013.

Neumark-Sztainer, D., Wall, M., Story, M., & Standish, A. R. (2012). Dieting and unhealthy weight control behaviors during adolescence: Associations with 10-year changes in body mass index. *Journal of Adolescent Health, 50*(10), 80–86. Retrieved from http://j.jadohealth.2011.05.010.

Pereira, M. A., Kartashov, A. I., Ebbeling, C. B., Van Horn, L., Slattery, M. L., Jacobs, D. R. Jr., & Ludwig, D. S. (2005). Fast-food habits, weight gain, and insulin resistance (the CARDIA study): 15-year prospective analysis. *The Lancet, 365*(9453), 36–42.

Pietiläinen, K. H., Saarni, S. E., Kaprio, J., & Rissanen, A. (2012). Does dieting make you fat? A twin study. *International Journal of Obesity, 36*(30), 456–464. Retrieved from http://doi.org/10.1038/ijo.2011.160.

Pingitore, R., Dugoni, B. L., Tindale, R. S., & Spring, B. (1994). Bias against overweight job applicants in a simulated employment interview. *Journal of Applied Psychology, 79*(6), 909–917. Retrieved from http://citeseerx.ist.psu.edu/viewdoc/download?doi=10.1.1.468.3727&rep=rep1&type=pdf.

Pi-Sunyer, W. (2014). The Look AHEAD trial: A review and discussion of its outcomes. *Current Nutrition Reports, 3*(4), 387–391. Retrieved from http://doi.org/10.1007/s13668-014-0099-x.

Puhl, R. M., Andreyeva, T., & Brownell, K. D. (2008). Perceptions of weight discrimination: Prevalence and comparison to race and gender discrimination in America. *International Journal of Obesity, 32*(6), 992–1000. Retrieved from http://doi.org/10.1038/ijo.2008.22.

Puhl, R. M., & Brownell, K. D. (2001). Bias, discrimination, and obesity. *Obesity Research, 9*(12), 788–805. Retrieved from http://doi.org/10.1038/oby.2001.108.

Puhl, R. M., & Brownell, K. D. (2006). Confronting and coping with weight stigma: An investigation of overweight and obese adults. *Obesity (Silver Spring), 14*(10), 1802–1815.

Puhl, R. M., & Heuer, C. A. (2009). The stigma of obesity: A review and update. *Obesity (Silver Spring), 17*(5), 941–964. Retrieved from http://doi.org/10.1038/oby.2006.208.

Puhl, R. M., & Heuer, C. A. (2010). Obesity stigma: Important considerations for public health. *American Journal of Public Health, 100*(6), 1019–1028. Retrieved from http://doi.org/10.2105/AJPH2009.159491.

Puhl, R. M., Heuer, C., & Sarda, V. (2011). Framing messages about weight discrimination: Impact on public support for legislation. *International Journal of Obesity, 25*, 863–872. Retrieved from http://doi.org/10.1038/ijo.2010.194.

Puhl, R. M., Wall, M. M., Chen, C., Austin, S. B., Eisenberg, M. E., & Neumark-Sztainer, D. (2017). Experiences of weight teasing in adolescence and weight-related outcomes in adulthood: A 15-year longitudinal study. *Preventive Medicine, 100*, 173–179. Retrieved from http://doi.org/10.1016/j.ypmed.2017.04.023.

Ricciardelli, L., McCabe, M., Holt, K., & Finemore, J. (2003). A biopsychosocial model for understanding body image and body change strategies among children. *Journal of Applied Developmental Psychology, 24*(4), 475–495. Retrieved from www.ncbi.nlm.nih.gov/pmc/articles/PMC2533817/.

Simon, G. E., Von Korff, M., Saunders, K., Miglioretti, D. L., Crane, P. K., van Belle, G., & Kessler, R. C. (2007). Association between obesity and psychiatric disorders in the U.S. adult population. *Archives of General Psychiatry, 63*(7), 824–830. Retrieved from http://doi.org/10.1001/archpsyc.63.7.824.

Slop-Op't Landt, M. C. T., van Further, E. F., van Beijsterveldt, C. E. M., Bartels, M., Willemsen, G., de Geus, E. J., . . . Boomsma, D. J. (2017). Prevalence of dieting and fear of weight gain across ages: A community sample from adolescents to the elderly. *International Journal of Public Health, 62*(8), 911–919. Retrieved from http://doi.org/10.1007/s00038-017-0948-7.

Smolak, L., Stiegel-Moore, R. H., & Levine, M. P. (Eds.). (1996). *The developmental psychopathology of eating disorders: Implications for research, prevention, and treatment.* New York, NY: Routledge.

Story, M., Rosenwinkel, K., Himes, J. H., Resnick, M. D., Harris, L. J., & Blum, R. W. (1991). Demographic and risk factors associated with chronic dieting in adolescents. *American Journal of Diseases of Children, 145*(9), 994–998.

Summerville, A. (1916). *Why be fat? Rules for weight-reduction and the preservation of youth and health.* New York, NY: Frederick A. Stokes Company.

Tsai, A. G., & Wadden, T. A. (2005). Systematic review: An evaluation of major commercial weight loss programs in the United States. *Annals of Internal Medicine, 142*(1), 56–66.

Tylka, T. L., Annunziato, R. A., Burgard, D., Daníelsdóttir, S., Shuman, E., Davis, C., & Calogero, R. M. (2014). The weight-inclusive versus weight-normative approach to health: Evaluating the evidence for prioritizing well-being over weight loss. *Journal of Obesity*, Article ID 983495, 18 pages. Retrieved from http://dx.doi.org/10.1155/2014/983495.

University of North Carolina at Chapel Hill. (2008, April 23). Three out of four American women have disordered eating, survey suggests. *Science News.* Retrieved from www.sciencedaily.com/releases/2008/04/080422202514.htm.

Unknown. *It doesn't make sense to call ourselves ugly.* Retrieved from https://adayinmyquotebook.com/2013/05/30/53013-it-doesnt-make-sense-to-call-ourselves-ugly/.

Vaughan, K., & Fouts, G. (2003). Changes in television and magazine exposure and eating disorder symptomatology. *Sex Roles, 49*(7–8), 313–320. Retrieved from http://doi.org/10.1023/A:1025103902708.

Wadden, T. A. (2006). The look AHEAD study: A description of the lifestyle intervention and the evidence supporting it. *Obesity (Silver Spring), 14*(5), 737–752. Retrieved from http://doi.org/10.1038/oby.2006.84.

Wolf, N. (1990). *The beauty myth.* Toronto, ON: Random House.

5

I Live Here and
I'll Decide
Treating Your Body as
Your Home

"I am drinking a lot of water, trying to distract myself when I feel like eating, counting calories, eating low-fat or nonfat meals and snacks, walking for a minimum of 30 minutes daily, taking the stairs whenever possible, and, of course, trying to visualize myself in a smaller body," I shared with my new therapist, Laura, at the start of our second session. I no longer drank excessively, but continued to binge eat or engage in cycles of grazing. I was beginning to realize the bingeing and grazing increased my distress, anxiety, and depression, and was ready to make changes.

I looked forward to working with Laura because she made me feel comfortable and she listened. In the short time I'd known her, she seemed to really understand where I was coming from regarding my issues with food and body. I expected Laura would lay out a plan and begin to hold me accountable for what I eat. I wanted someone to push and encourage me to finally lose weight and keep it off.

"I think what we are talking about is binge eating disorder," Laura explained after she completed the assessment questions. "It's about your relationship with food and *why* you binge eat, not your weight."

What? How can it not be about my weight? Maybe I misread Laura. How could I, someone who is fat with no willpower, have an eating disorder? I've done Weight Watchers, Jenny Craig, Physicians Weight Loss, and countless weight management programs affiliated with hospitals and physicians. Obviously, something is wrong with me because while I always lose weight on these programs, I can't keep it off.

"What would it be like to be in this same body for the remainder of your life?" she asked.

I felt a rush of emotion come over me and wanted to run out of Laura's office. My heart began to pound, and I questioned why I thought a therapist was a good idea to address my weight. No previous therapist had ever suggested anything like this before and I could not imagine someone in their right mind thinking this could be an acceptable approach to my problems. After all, if I finally conquered my weight, things would likely fall in line in the other areas of my life. I'd feel more confident in my work and relationships, and I'd be healthier.

"I can't imagine living in this body for the rest of my life," I replied honestly to Laura's question. "Plus, being fat isn't healthy, so I need to lose weight." How could it be possible for someone who is fat and about to turn 30 to have an eating disorder? Only teenage girls who starve themselves get eating disorders.

This woman asked me to give up and accept that I am fat. How could this help me? Maybe she sensed I was ready to give up? It was true. I had grown tired of fighting my weight. Tired of the comments by family and friends, and not feeling worthy of career opportunities or love interests. Tired of being so critical of myself and watching life pass me by.

I'm not a loser and I'm not giving up. I had to convince Laura that I was ready to do something about my weight. I began to explain why this time I am in it for the long haul and am dedicated to doing whatever I have to do when Laura stopped me.

"What if a part of ending the distress with your body is to stop dieting? What if I told you that this never-ending cycle of losing and regaining weight is part of the eating disorder? What if I told you that you are perfect the way you are?"

I looked at Laura and began to sob. Somehow, I knew she was right. There is a part of me that questioned my inner critic. I have done everything possible to keep that internal voice at bay. *I don't want her to win this battle. I want her to go away because there is nothing in this world I want more than to be thin.*

I left the session reeling and immediately began to think about what to eat. I knew a binge would be inevitable and felt frustrated there were no drive-thru restaurants close to Laura's office. I drove fast around the D.C. beltway to my neighborhood in Alexandria, where I pulled into a McDonalds and ordered a cheeseburger and fries. It went down quickly and calmed me.

Laura and I spent many subsequent sessions talking about where I am now and how far I've come since the first time I sought therapy 6 years ago. I continued to resist the idea I would never lose weight, but I gained a sense of my own resilience. I came to understand how the development of an eating disorder protected me during my childhood when I needed survival strategies to fend for myself in the chaotic world of the adults around me. Eating in secret gave me relief from the uncertainty of whether I could depend on my parents and other adults to keep me safe or attend to my needs. It allowed me to temporarily not feel the anxiety my mind could not ignore, much like a shoe rubbing an open sore on a long walk.

It made sense that parts of me were smart enough to figure out I needed something to help me deal with situations over which I had no control and evoked fear. Bingeing and grazing were wonderful distractors, but they were only a piece of the puzzle and often, they led to further problems. I would have to deal with my hatred of my body and how my feelings about it maintained the eating disorder. I continued in therapy with Laura, and participated in group therapy, too.

"Your body size is exactly what I am afraid of and the reason I can't get well." The words seemed to float out of the emaciated figure sitting across from me. They registered so slowly it was as if I could see the words linger in the air. They hovered as I tried to decide if I wanted to allow my tears to flow or give in to the impulse to say something nasty in response.

Annie was part of a body image group made up of Laura's clients. She reminded the group every time we meet that she is scared to get well because she fears looking like those of us who are in higher weight bodies.

"I'm tired of being your worst fear Annie," I said through my tears. "We are all in the same boat. We all have eating disorders and we all hate our bodies. I would give anything to be thin like you, but if I focus on that I am never going to move past this bullshit and have a life." I realized, for the first time that evening, that like Annie, I focused on weight as the centerpiece of the eating disorder. I recognized her fear when she talked about her body and understood she was exhausted by the fight. I finally understood in that moment that I would have to address the internalized distress I spent years trying to silence differently. I could not depend on changing the size of my body as a means to an end.

▶ SHAME AND BLAME

Dieting is the most potent political sedative in women's history.
—Naomi Wolf

Women's body image is a collective issue. Our society suffers when half the population channels their creative energy into being smaller.
—Melissa Toler

For many people with binge eating disorder, a primary motivation for entering treatment is to lose weight (or stop weight gain). Binge eating distresses people most because of body shame, and less so for the distance it creates from fully experiencing their lives, numbing their feelings and shutting down their desires. Both dieting and being thin feel *essential* for self-worth and positive body image, sometimes above all else. And when a person binges, they blame themselves for being fat and lacking the necessary "willpower" to lose weight and keep it off.

Back in the mid-eighties, Dr. Albert Stunkard of the University of Pennsylvania challenged the assumption that weight is determined by diet and behavior (Wadden & Stunkard, 1986). His study of adopted children and weight demonstrated a strong correlation between the body mass index (BMI) of biological parents and adoptees. There was no statistical relationship between the BMI of adoptive parents and adoptees, suggesting environment has little or no effect. In other words, body size and shape may be determined largely by genetics. Most of us need only look at family members to see some truth to this assertion. Yet, we persevere with the notion that thin is necessarily appropriate, and achievable, for everyone.

Additionally, we believe our body cannot be trusted to maintain a "healthy" weight; our so-called failed efforts to maintain weight loss seem to support this conclusion. As a result of such self-blame, millions of us hand over decision making about food and exercise to alleged experts. We are willing to try almost anything. In fact, the total U.S. weight loss market is estimated at $66.3 billion for 2016. Regardless of the 95 percent failure rate for long-term weight loss, we blame ourselves for the "failure" of not being thin. And the most effective marketing tool of all? Shame. One of my clients notes in a journal entry, "I don't feel safe or comfortable in my body. I hate my body. I want it to be different. All the time. It has never, ever, been right."

▶ THE DIETING DILEMMA

Our bodies respond to food restriction as an immediate threat. When we restrict food by ignoring hunger cues, our bodies begin to protect themselves in a number of ways. This is a natural and valuable reaction; indeed, the body doesn't know the difference between a famine and a diet. When on a low-calorie diet, our brain responds by releasing neurotransmitters that drive us to focus on food. The brain tries to get us to do whatever is necessary to obtain nourishment. Some studies suggest that when we are on a restrictive diet, the brain may make us focus on foods that are the most quickly digested, such as highly refined carbohydrates (Massey & Hill, 2012). These tend to be the very foods we forbid ourselves on a diet, which further intensifies the craving.

> It's a Dr Pepper every day. Because not having it feels weird. Feels untethered. Feels like I'm just being good, because everyone knows soda is the root of all evil. But I love Dr Pepper. It's part of me. And it tastes good. Even when I'm full, or I'm having a sugar rush—or a sugar crash—I still drink it. It's being in the drive-thru line and thinking—completely certain—I'll get a small, or a medium, and five seconds later ordering a large. Where did that come from? I wasn't going to do that this time. Why did I just do that? It's hating myself for not having

any self-control, for splurging. It's committing that this time will be different. This time I'll do better. This time I'll stop myself. And it never happens.

Ninety-five percent of dieters go "off" their diet within 4 months. Being "off" a diet often means overeating at a time the body is in nutrition panic mode, storing all it can. Thus, weight gain following a diet is fast and furious, more so than prior to dieting. This rapid weight gain is often what precipitates another attempt at dieting, and the cycle begins again. But, these are our body's efforts to simply keep us alive in a time of perceived threat. Our body is doing what BED often serves to do in situations of complex trauma: allow us to survive.

> The beginning of my disordered eating as a child and teen was not only around bingeing. I starved myself purposefully in hopes of losing weight. I thought nothing of it. I never imagined I was harming myself—getting thin was healthy, right? When I was in high school I wouldn't eat anything all day—not even snacks. I never ate one meal in my high school cafeteria. I would eat nothing from the night before until I got home from school the next day around 3 p.m. and then I would raid the refrigerator and cupboards and eat whatever I could find. Then I'd eat dinner with my family, which was a stressful event with my rage-aholic father holding court at the table only wanting the attention of my mother and silence from us kids. I had terrible headaches and developed anemia as a result of this eating pattern. I'm sure my metabolism took a hit, too. No one ever questioned what I was doing. My parents seemed oblivious, because they were.

▶ IN THE BEGINNING

Early on in our lives, we are strongly attuned to our physical experience of the world, aware of our immediate needs for food, touch, and safety. When we experienced a need and made our caregivers aware of it, if they were able to respond *most* of the time, we felt attached to them, and safe. When this is the case, we learn over time that the world is basically OK, we will survive when needs are not met perfectly, and that we can count on others. This directly translates to our "felt" sense. When our body is primarily a source of information about the environment around us, we trust it. However, when the body tells us one thing but caregivers and culture tell another, we come to learn that our body is not to be believed. Repeated diet failures serve to reinforce this conclusion, and thus we buy what the weight loss industry intends to sell, with little or no challenge to the validity or veracity of its claims.

▶ WORTHY AS YOUR HOME

Although we don't often consider it, our body does its very best for us 24 hours a day, 365 days a year, despite the damage we may inflict on it or the feelings of shame our narratives about it elicit. Our bodies tirelessly offer extraordinary amounts of information about our needs for both survival and pleasure. Our body is the source of our intuition, and does its best to let us know what works for its care and well-being. It is a core part of the work of recovery to begin to listen to this information effectively, and learn how to respond with compassion and wisdom.

The fourth practice—take back your body as your home—is central to long-term recovery from BED. Parallel to the rest of the work of healing, the ways we care for our body must be increasingly rooted in *protection and compassion*, not fear and shame. Care needs to come from seeing our body as our *home*, as our means of moving through and experiencing the world, not as a billboard for approval from others. Our body allows us to connect with the whole world around us, to see, hear, feel and touch, to hug our children, to ride our horses and pet our dogs, to share our inner world with others. It allows us to process what we experience, and advocate for change. It is our felt sense that literally allows us to feel love and empathy for others. It allows us a place to survive until we are able to heal from past hurts. Our body is both resilient and fragile, and *regardless of size or shape*, worth the very best care we can offer. Any other message is a product of shame, not truth.

▶ WHAT ABOUT WEIGHT?

The true indicators of health and longevity may surprise you. A weight at which your body is happy is *not*:

- ▶ A single unchanging number on a scale

- ▶ A body mass index (BMI) category

▶ A specific shape

▶ A specific size of clothing

▶ Readily controllable

▶ A measure of willpower

▶ Easily known/calculated

A good weight for one's body cannot be determined without taking into consideration genetic makeup and lived experience with food and weight over time, something BMI and diets simply do not do.

BMI derives from an almost 200-year-old classification system initially intended to assess whole populations of people, not individuals. In the latter half of the last century, it morphed into something used by the insurance industry to estimate mortality rates and "health risks" based on height and weight from aggregated data. Indeed, BMI profoundly favors insurance companies, who use the index to determine rates for life insurance and health care premiums. Research clearly shows using BMI to determine mortality risks is misguided. A meta-analysis of 97 studies with a total of almost 3 million people as research subjects published in the *Journal of the American Medical Association* showed that people who fall into the "overweight" category actually live longest (Flegal et. al., 2013).

When it comes to body shape, even the commonly used waist circumference measurement as an indicator of health isn't valid, according to Flegal and Graubard (2009). The hypothesis was that women should not measure more than 35 inches around the waist, 40 inches for men. In this study of thousands of Americans, researchers found "having a higher number for any measure of body shape or size, or body composition, is not predictive of higher risks of dying from all causes compared to people with 'healthy' numbers and picture-perfect bodies." Once again, the data do not support the stories we have been asked to believe.

In fact, the research we have to date suggests weight is both surprisingly variable and not easy to influence. As there are many natural variations across humans in things like eye and hair color, skin pigmentation, height, and length of feet, so too is the nature of weight and shape. "Healthy" weight is actually quite different than we have been led to believe. It is:

- ▶ Individual and often variable

- ▶ Impacted by many factors, both individual and environmental (including access to nutrient-rich foods, disease, genetics, environment, age, composition of gut bacteria, exposure to hormone-disrupting chemicals, metabolism, stress levels, and trauma)

- ▶ Not necessarily indicative of disease or pathology

- ▶ Largely predetermined by genetics

- ▶ Highly resistant to long-term change

Your weight is not a moral failing (or "success" if you lose weight) and may not even necessarily be a health problem, but instead the result of a complex cluster of factors that may or may not change over time. Research increasingly suggests a focus on making compassionate attuned choices for your body offers much more promise for well-being than directed efforts to lose weight.

▶ THE FOURTH PRACTICE: ATTUNED EATING AND MOVEMENT

In my own recovery and in working with many clients over the years, I have developed a way of attending to our bodies that I call Attuned Eating and Movement (AEM). AEM is an approach to health based on the premise that attunement to our whole body—the "felt sense"—offers a much better path toward recovery and well-being. AEM incorporates many of the same tenets as recovery from the shame of trauma, and thus it reinforces and validates the rest of recovery work. Healing your relationship with your body parallels healing your relationship with yourself and others. Interestingly, one recent study found the expression of thoughts, feelings, or needs is a *critical aspect of eating from body cues*. The suppression of your voice may decrease your trust in internal signals of hunger and fullness. Attuned eating occurs with high levels of emotional awareness and low levels of self-silencing. Indeed, healing your body by listening to it parallels all the work of recovery.

As part of BED treatment, AEM reduces binge eating and weight cycling, diminishes the physical and psychological effects of shame and self-blame, and improves body image. As we will see, using POWR with AEM makes for a very effective combination. AEM invites:

▶ A shift from external rules for eating/movement to reliance on internal cues, making choices from a combination of current desire, past body experience, and "big picture" nutrition

▶ A focus on "curiosity and course correction"

▶ A focus on providing the best possible care for one's *current* body

▶ Allowing our weight to be determined by our body's wisdom

These concepts may seem very difficult to embrace initially. When change around body and eating feels impossible, I often ask my clients: Would you want the people you love to embrace these tenets for their own bodies? If so, then why would you have a different set of rules for you than for those you love if not because of old (untrue) stories? Our job is to move in this direction, one step at a time, with the support of treatment and others in recovery. It is not a landing place, but an ongoing process. Thankfully, moving toward the *whole truth* is something most people with BED have been trying to do for a long time.

Remember: *BED recovery involves binge eating.* This is not failure. Learning forensically from binge eating is critical to the process of AEM and healing itself. In fact, some degree of going to food to soothe may always be in your "toolbox." I often tell my clients to never waste a binge; always learn from the experience. Wise words from a client of mine:

> I accept that sometimes the skills and insights of recovery will be no
> match for the strength and depth of certain emotional reactions. At
> such times, I might return to what works. Chocolate almonds have been
> amazingly helpful for me in times of stress. So, in the face of a binge,
> I don't judge myself. I try to be patient, kind, and compassionate.

Learn what you can from the inevitable bumps in the road, and just keep on driving.

▶ FROM OUR OWN WISDOM

Many of my clients are convinced—as was I—that if they trusted their body, their eating and weight would be out of control. In fact, the opposite appears to be true. A growing body of research shows when you allow yourself the food and movement your body truly wants most of the time, well-being improves and binge eating decreases. Of additional benefit, when you eat and move in response to physical needs, you feel less body shame. You feel more satisfied, and more at home in your body.

The basics of attuned eating involve doing what your body already knows how to do. Even if you may have ignored body cues for years or tried to silence them with willpower, they will still be available.

1. Use POWR to connect with the "felt sense" of body needs

2. Leave morality out of food and weight

3. Discover the critical nature of satiety

4. Build body wisdom over time

5. Do what you can: from scarcity to sufficiency

6. Allow your body to determine your weight

Let's look at each of these basic components in turn. We will begin with the use of POWR in attuned eating. The remaining steps allow you to challenge the whole diet and weight loss paradigm, and decide what the real truth is for your unique body.

▶ POWR AND ATTUNED EATING

Whenever you feel the desire to eat, POWR invites you to slow down and check in to determine if your current need is really for food or for something else, and how to make choices to best meet the actual need. POWR brings the opportunity to actively choose what you want to do. It might mean eating, it might mean bingeing even, or it might mean something else entirely.

The first invitation, "pause into presence," asks that you simply check in to awareness of your body in the present moment, to the "felt sense." You might want to do some square breathing to bring your attention to your body.

To "open and allow," simply attend to what is happening. What do you feel in your body? It is important to learn your unique physical cues for hunger. Can you identify the sensations of hunger? Such sensations may vary at different levels of hunger, ranging from a slight feeling of emptiness in the stomach and perhaps some thoughts about food, to stomach growling and trouble focusing on other things. Bring your attention to any thoughts you may have about eating right now. What are the messages you hear? Are you judging your hunger? Are you telling yourself you should not be hungry now, or that you should wait to eat until the "right time"?

If you are not sensing hunger, the desire for food might come from a part that is experiencing fear or shame, and is seeking soothing or distraction. See if you can employ POWR as described in Chapter 3 to determine what the real need might be. Remember, if you ultimately chose to go to food, be kind to yourself afterward. See if you can go back to the POWR process and meet the real need then.

If you sense hunger, move on to "wisely consider." What you would like to eat right now? What sounds good to you (salty, sweet, hot or cold, creamy or crunchy)? How would you like to feel at the end of this snack/meal? Light and ready to go, or more substantially full and sated? If you don't have access to the perfect fit, what might be a satisfactory substitute? Can you get the desired food sometime soon?

Finally, respond with care. Try and eat what sounds good to you right now, as best you are able. Try not to eat something because you *should* eat it. Eat what you desire and see how it makes your body feel. Try to really tune in to desire. Assume you could have any food you wish, without guilt or shame. Might you want ice cream? Stir fry? A brownie or a burger? A mango? Notice when your body has had enough. How can you tell? What are your unique cues of satisfaction and fullness?

Eating without distraction is important, especially as you are learning your body's cues. It is one of the hardest behavioral changes to make. Often there is a powerful connection between eating and watching TV, being on the computer, or some other activity. Eating without distractions may feel weird, wrong, and even scary initially. We will discuss more about this change at the end of this chapter. If you notice fear in response to eating without distraction, try using the POWR process with that fear too; what is the real issue at play if you remain tuned in when you eat? If you choose to eat with distraction, that's fine.

▶ LEAVE MORALITY OUT OF FOOD

Do you feel better about yourself if you eat carrots instead of cake? Do you feel less anxious and ashamed if you have a "good" day and stick to your food plan? When you give in to the desire to eat something forbidden by the plan, do you feel like you are "cheating"? The messages around us about foods are ubiquitous and conflicting. Gluten is bad. Sugar is bad. Kale will save your life. Gluttony is a sin. We should "detoxify" and "cleanse" our bodies. When eating certain foods is associated with your moral character, you judge yourself harshly and amplify the judgments of others against you, especially if you have committed the sin of not being thin.

People eat all kinds of foods for all kinds of reasons, including joy, celebration, community, availability, access, and nutritional needs. What you eat and how much you eat is not statement about your self-worth. When you reject such a paradigm, food can be food. It will satisfy you or it won't. You will have what you'd like or you won't. It will sit well with your body or it won't. There is nothing else at stake other than an opportunity to learn more about your body or your current circumstance.

▶ THE CRITICAL NATURE OF SATIETY

Satiety refers to the combination of having *enough* food and having food you *desire*. If you are fortunate enough to have access to foods you love, satiety can be a very powerful tool in BED recovery, especially in the beginning. Allowing yourself the food you really want in the moment is especially healing, both to your body and to your sense of deserving to have your needs met. Over time, as you build trust in meeting your needs, you can defer your desire until it's convenient without triggering a feeling of scarcity.

Consider foods you only eat when you binge, or allow yourself only if you are "cheating" on your diet. What do you believe might happen if you were to allow yourself access to these foods? Do you fear you might never stop eating them? Has that ever actually happened? Even in the worst binge, when you are *deliberately* paying no attention to your cues, eating eventually stops. Imagine if you knew you could have cookies whenever you wanted them—would you stop eating them sooner? If you know it won't be the last time you eat cookies, do you feel the urge as strongly to eat them all until they are gone? Consider trying this approach with just one of the foods you forbid yourself. Be sure it is the food you truly desire. Don't eat vanilla if you really want chocolate. Don't eat cheese flavored rice cakes when you really want Doritos. And don't eat ice cream if you really want a salad.

Many health experts get a bit horrified at this suggestion. Binge foods are often highly processed, laden with chemicals, and may offer limited nutritional value. Some foods may even be chemically manipulated to continue to taste good for longer than they otherwise might. So, how in good conscience can I recommend you eat these foods in recovery? Believe it or not, when all food is allowed (assuming we have access to nutrition-packed foods, too), we come to see that our bodies actually do not feel best eating highly processed, nutrient-poor foods more than occasionally.

Food is medicine. While no one would argue that nutritional needs are irrelevant to making good food choices, I would suggest we must remember that for those with BED, food is charged with emotion and meaning that must be addressed *first and foremost*. As such, making peace with trigger foods, and removing their enormous psychological charge, is critical to truly be tuned in to the body's *actual* desire for these foods. Thus, when we can truly decide what we want from a place of body wisdom, that Dorito can be just a Dorito.

> I finally rejected the notion of good and bad foods. Before starting BED recovery though, my dieter mentality definitely compartmentalized foods as okay and not okay to eat. I remember when I was a college student working at a hospital, I was so proud of myself for never buying anything out of the vending machines, even if I was hungry,

because that was all bad food. Thinking of food this way was constant
for me. It was automatic. It's taken a lot of work and time to change
my way of thinking.

It is important to note here that AEM assumes significant privilege. When
you can't buy food that sounds good, or can't buy enough food to eat until
you're full, when you can't afford or have access to nutrient dense foods, or
have to choose between rent and buying fresh vegetables, AEM is far more
difficult to implement. This is where it becomes culturally critical to address
the increasing problem of food insecurity. People with BED have an even
more difficult recovery road when they do not have access to foods their
bodies enjoy most.

▶ BUILD BODY WISDOM OVER TIME

There is much information to be gleaned by paying attention to your physical body. How do various foods make your body feel? Light? Heavy? Do
any foods cause bloating or heartburn? What makes you feel well-fed; what
leaves you feeling empty? What gives you energy? What saps energy? When
do you like to eat? How does your body feel at the end of a given meal?

Do you typically eat from a schedule, or structure with your eating in some
other way? Do you ever eat with little expectation about when the next
time will be? Or perhaps some of both? When you start listening to the
physical signals, whatever timetable or meal structure (if any) your body
desires will become clear. You may find your body does well most days
with three meals and three snacks. Or mostly snacking throughout the
day. Or a bigger breakfast and smaller dinner. You may enjoy a snack at
bedtime, and eat less at dinner. You may discover that protein for breakfast
is essential to your ability to feel sated and focused for the morning's work.
You may discover that no rules works best for you. The bottom line is that
tending to your body's needs effectively requires adaptability, validation,
practice, and trust.

Eating well means paying attention to the big picture of your overall nutrition and your unique needs, as well as the small picture of your in-the-
moment desires. It is a balancing act, ongoing and adaptive. It is not a
problem to be solved, but something to be tended. It may be helpful to work

with your therapist or nutrition professional on the specifics. Resources are also included at the end of this chapter.

Again, there is no right choice. It is OK to eat waffles, even though they may make you sleepy. You may not wish to do so on a Monday morning before a big meeting. Is it OK to still overeat? Of course. Everyone does, on occasion, if they have access to adequate food. And you may overeat sometimes seeking comfort. It will be less and less often as time passes, less food at a sitting, and less dissociation when it happens. You will come back to self-awareness sooner, and deal with the reason for seeking food with more compassion than shame.

▶ WHAT ABOUT EXERCISE?

There are as many messages about exercise as there are about food choices: how much, how often, and why you *must* do it. Exercising, like food, has taken on moral connotations. If you don't do it, it says something about a lack of personal integrity or responsibility. You feel less OK about yourself if you miss a workout or exercise less than you should.

As noted earlier, shame certainly sells, and the fitness industry is no exception to the rule. Revenue in 2014 was $24.2 billion, a sharp 7.4 percent increase over 2013. Seems we are all supposed to be jumping on the proverbial treadmill, or we risk untoned calves, a life of ill health, and certain death. We don't actually know for sure what the optimal amount of exercise is for any given person, nor do we know the impact of movement on health for any individual. But, we do have research results on the relationship between weight and exercise, and they may surprise you.

In a review of exercise intervention studies, researchers followed people training for marathons, sedentary young twins, and post-menopausal "overweight" and "obese" women (based on BMI) who increased physical activity through running, cycling, or personal training sessions. Most people in these studies typically only lost a few pounds, even under highly controlled scenarios where their diets were kept constant. Other meta-analyses, which looked at a number of exercise studies, have come to similarly conclusions about exercise as a method for losing weight (Thomas et al., 2012).

Exercise accounts for only a small portion of daily calorie burn. According to Herman Pontzer, an anthropologist and researcher at Hunter College in New York, "exercise is only around 10 to 30 percent of total energy expenditure (depending on the person and excluding professional athletes that workout as a job). It is very difficult to create a caloric deficit through exercise." According to the NIH's Kevin Hall, if a hypothetical 200-pound man added *60 minutes* of medium intensity running four days per week while keeping his calorie intake the same, and he did this for 30 days, he'd lose five pounds (as cited in Pontzer, 2017). "If this person decided to increase food intake or relax more to recover from the added exercise, then even less weight would be lost," Hall added. This may well be the result of the body conserving energy by slowing metabolism when it perceives additional energy might be needed for threats to survival.

It may also be, as some studies suggest, that energy expenditure reaches a plateau. After adjusting for body size and composition, another study by Herman Pontzer et al. (2012), which tracked 332 adults from Ghana, South Africa, Seychelles, Jamaica, and the United States, found "total energy expenditure was positively correlated with physical activity, but the relationship was markedly stronger over the lower range of physical activity." He calls this the constrained model of energy expenditure, which suggests the effect of physical activity on the human body is not linear. In light of our evolutionary history—when food sources were less reliable—he argues the body sets a limit on how much energy it is willing to expend, regardless of how active we may be. "The overarching idea," Pontzer explained, "is that the body is trying to defend a particular energy expenditure level no matter how active you get." It appears, after a certain amount of exercise, you don't keep burning calories at the same rate. More exercise will not, in fact, mean more weight lost.

▶ IF NOT TO LOSE WEIGHT, WHY DO IT?

So much of the joy of movement has been lost for people with BED. For many of my clients, movement is often reduced to exercise in pursuit of a goal of weight loss or shape change. For most of us humans however, our bodies simply enjoy (and significantly benefit from) movement, *regardless of weight change*. A systematic review of longitudinal studies suggests movement provides a range of benefits, including reducing blood pressure and triglycerides in the blood, as well as reducing Type 2 diabetes, stroke, and heart attack (Reiner, Niermann, Jekauc, & Woll, 2013). Studies have also shown people who exercise are at a lower risk of developing cognitive impairment from Alzheimer's and dementia. They also score higher on cognitive ability tests. Movement releases endorphins and reduces cortisol, both of which work to lessen the experience of anxiety and stress (Reiner et al., 2013).

There are even more benefits to be had from movement, beyond physical health. When you make movement choices your own again, based on your body's responses to it, you validate your desire for life and for living. Moving heals body shame narratives. When you move as you desire, you can feel the joy in a moment again because you are actually *present* in it.

> I remember the trampoline as a child. I was flying. My body loved it! I felt light and strong. I couldn't get enough. I cannot believe how I felt when I got on my daughter's trampoline. It was like stepping back into physical joy. I was jumping and crying. It was there all along, but I couldn't allow it from the fear of someone laughing at me. Recovery is helping me put my joy above my fear.

▶ RECLAIMING SEXUALITY

Movement you enjoy is also a gentle way back to reclaiming your sexual energy. For many with BED, sexual trauma changed everything about being in touch with the body. Damage can be done by physical boundary violation of course, but also by emotional and psychological bullying and cultural messages of sexual objectification. Such messages make women's bodies the property of others. Out of fear or shame (or both), many with BED disconnect from sensations of sexual desire. For some with BED, high weight may feel like protection from sexual advances.

> Every time I went on a diet and lost weight, I got scared. Seeing my body get smaller made me think I had to change everything about how I behaved. I had to look a certain way, be flirtatious, and never say no. When I was fat, I allowed myself to say no because I told myself no one wanted me. I gave being fat the power to let me uphold my boundaries. Actually, I met my partner when I was fat. But I was well

into recovery, and heard my sexual voice by then. I learn every day that
I don't have to change my body at all. I just have to reclaim my own
space, no matter my size.

The work of recovery means you learn you do not have to fit into the social
and cultural definitions of what is sexually attractive to actually *be* sexually
attractive. Quite to the contrary, recovery is about claiming and honoring
your sexual self, *as is.*

For people with histories of sexual trauma, especially as children, it is
important to remember that such experiences often link sexuality to danger,
powerlessness, and betrayal. Indeed, our "fight/flight/freeze/fawn" mechanism may trigger when we experience sexual arousal. Much of the work
of healing is in the disconnection of threat and danger from our healthy
sexuality, allowing our powerful Self to protect and soothe when we become
hijacked by younger parts. There is absolutely no shame in this reaction to
sexuality; it is our exactly how we are wired to respond. The true loss here
is that sexual desire, as with desires for food or movement, should be safe,
authentic, and pleasurable. Often, there has been limited opportunity for a
healthy sexual self to develop. Recovery work can allow that development to
finally take place safely, learning that our bodies deserve access to whatever
our individual sexual needs might be.

It is important to know that, for people who have been sexually harmed,
physically or psychologically, the process of healing may or may not ultimately include a sexual partner. This is not a failure, nor does it mean that
you cannot recover from BED. It may mean you choose to grieve the loss of
this kind of intimacy, and find other ways to be close to safe others. Allow
yourself, as with food and movement, to find your own path. Focus on the
next step in the journey, not the horizon.

An additional form of sexual trauma, weight stigma tells us that only thin
people are sexy, or even sexual. Almost all the mass media images we see
of "sexy" women (and increasingly men too) are unrealistic, and objectify
specific body parts. Look around you. People of all sizes are loved and in
sexual relationships. A very big part of recovery is slowly, and usually with
the support of treatment, taking judgment of your body back from systems
and industries that rely on these absurd cultural standards. Sexuality should
feel safe, fun, and under your control. If you have dealt with sexual trauma,

or have strong feelings of fear or shame about sexuality and your body, be sure your treatment provider is comfortable working on these issues. They are critical in healing your relationship with your body.

If you are a nonheterosexual person (lesbian, gay, bisexual, transgender, non-binary, gender-fluid, asexual, and many other identifications), you have another system of stigma intersecting with weight bias. Claiming your sexual identity in a society that marginalizes and stigmatizes those who do not fit in rigid binary categories is difficult enough, but weight and shape stigma add to this challenge. Community building and advocacy here are critical to recovery, especially when your treatment team may not have expertise in both BED treatment and issues of gender and/or sexual orientation. Most important to remember here: the shame and fear you feel are not about your sexuality or sexual orientation, or your body itself. They are about stigma and social constructs based in historical prejudice and oppression, not truth.

POWR can be a helpful tool in this process too. Fear and shame associated with sensuality and sexuality often trigger a desire to go to food to soothe and distract. Remember, your compassionate adult Self is naturally committed to never place a young, scared part of you in danger, nor will your Self enter into a sexual relationship without proper safeguards in place, protecting your young parts from harm. While reclaiming your sexual Self may require dealing with strong emotions and somatic sensations, POWR can help you define what you need to allow an intimate relationship with a trusted partner (should you wish for one), discovering pleasure and connection on your own terms.

▶ FROM OUR OWN WISDOM: ATTUNED MOVEMENT

Moving from attuned wisdom can also be explored with the POWR process. Attuned movement invites us to do the following:

- ▶ Move when your body desires

- ▶ Move in the ways your body desires

- ▶ Stop moving when your body is done

- ▶ Do it again when you feel the need or desire

▶ Learn your body's movement needs over time (they may ebb and flow)

▶ Keep to your own truths about movement; stay away from the "should" messages

▶ Know it is OK to not have a strong desire for movement and to consider a "movement as medicine" approach

Learning when your body wants to move takes time and practice. Desire to move might actually feel like fatigue. Or it might feel like restlessness or muscle tightness. You might yawn a lot when you need to move, or feel bored and unfocused. See what changes if you stretch a bit, or dance a little, or take a short walk.

Remember, not wanting to move is *not* pathological. It's ok to not be an athlete by nature; many people are not. You may also be in need of rest or sleep deprived. Most of us struggle with less than adequate sleep in our lives; your body may be in need of restoration and recuperation. When we are tired, cues of all kinds (physical, emotional) are harder to access, and we are more easily hijacked by overwhelmed parts. There is no shame in resting; it is part of the work of recovery.

If indeed you do like to move (most of us actually do), what types of movement do you enjoy? Try taking the weight loss parameters off when considering what defines movement. Do you enjoy walking, gardening, or tap dancing? Lifting weights? Playing soccer? Yoga? Playing with the dog? Swimming? Raking the leaves? Painting the bedroom? Think of times of joy when moving. What were you doing? What made them enjoyable? Your body may enjoy many types and intensities of movement. Try to allow them to be equal psychologically. See what you really want. Your body may not be able to move in certain ways because of illness, chronic pain, or physical ability. Or, you may not have access to places that are safe to move, or access to equipment that works for your body shape, size or ability. It can also be very difficult with limited financial resources, erratic or long work hours, or childcare responsibilities to find opportunity or energy for movement. We must do what we are able, finding options and compromise as best we can. The rest is the work of advocacy for inclusivity and cultural change.

Given these limitations, whenever possible, allow yourself in-the-moment decisions when it comes to movement. Your needs for movement may vary from day to day, week to week. You may wish to incorporate movement several days in a row and then take a break. You might move more in summer than winter, or vary as you have more or less time. You may notice benefits to your mood and body if you get a certain amount of movement in your life, and may try to make that happen when possible. Try to allow the choice for movement in one day to be independent of the next day. You are no longer moving with an expectation of weight loss, but rather making movement part of your self-care. Most critically, the amount of movement you do is unrelated to success or failure in your recovery. *In fact, if you never work out again, you are exactly as OK as if you move daily.* There will be some differences to your physical and mental health based on your movement decisions, but they do not make you a better or worse person, or your body more or less worthy of whatever care you can offer.

What if you're not a big movement person? Suppose it feels like work, another expectation you can't meet? Suppose this: you don't *have* to do anything. The choice of when and how much to move belongs to you and your life circumstances. It is OK to think of movement as "medicine" for your body, and do it for that reason alone. We do know that movement, for most people, has major benefits for staying strong and able-bodied as long as possible. You may wish simply to identify ways to help make your body more functional for daily life; that is, do enough movement so you are able to walk up a flight of stairs without getting winded or experience less pain when carrying grocery bags or standing for work. This is a fine motivation for movement.

I have found for many of my clients, it is a combination of reasons to move that sustains them over the long term. Some movement they love to do, some they do for the benefits, like weight lifting to build strength. Sometimes they do it frequently, sometimes less so. Ultimately, whatever the type or frequency of movement in BED recovery, the motivation needs to come from care and protection for your body as your home.

▶ COMMON CHALLENGES TO AEM

Changing cognitive and behavioral patterns, especially those connected to soothing or distraction, feels incredibly difficult initially. You feel a powerful pull to do exactly the opposite of what you know is self-care. This is not pathology or lack of inner strength. It is how you are wired to cope with old dangers. Binge eating has become essentially automatic when you feel fear or shame. The neurological response to soothe and escape is a habit established over many years. This is why most people with BED are very resistant to eating without distraction. Checking out with food feels safer than staying present. It is a direct, literal challenge to the core behavior we have gone to for a sense of safety for years. However, the truth is this: checking out is not *safe*. In fact, it is rather like walking out into the street without looking. Fortunately, our brain can create new neural pathways, and we can create a new normal. Every time you do something other than binge, you strengthen new connections in the brain. Every time you choose to stop and go through the POWR process *before* turning to food or away from movement, you contribute to transformation. *The urge to binge will pass.* After it does, you will feel the psychological and somatic reward of relief for staying with your true needs and not harming yourself with food. This helps to reinforce and sustain the new pattern.

▶ POINTERS

I asked my clients to tell me any important pointers to share with readers of this book that they found especially helpful in their shift to AEM. Here are some of their thoughts.

1. Begin each time you eat with grounding into presence.

2. Define the patterns of binge eating for you so you know what to expect. (When? Where? Time of day? Place? Foods? With anyone? With any distractions?)

3. Expect trigger times and ask for support if you can. Make a quick change (sit somewhere else to eat, listen to the radio instead of watching TV, watch something different, eat outside).

4. Eat more often throughout the day; don't get too hungry (less is not virtuous).

5. Eat binge foods at non-binge times, as you desire them.

6. Stay checked in (PIES) throughout day.

7. Use POWR when the urge to binge hits.

8. Distract for a bit if nothing else is working. Change where you are (go outside, stretch, spend time with a pet). Come back to yourself and try POWR when you can.

9. Start the practice of eating without distraction at easier times (perhaps breakfast or a snack at work).

10. Know this will be a slow process of change. There are no "21 days to freedom" or "ten simple steps." Change needs to be slow and gentle.

11. Eating to soothe may always remain in your toolbox. You don't need to have "the last binge of your life" thinking. Decide if you really need to use that tool right now, and if so, how much is enough?

12. Checking out from our stressful lives for a time is healthy and reasonable. If you want to check out, can you do it in any other way? Suppose you just allow yourself to take a break.

13. Be extra gentle with yourself and your body following a bump in the recovery road.

14. Always celebrate any effort to take better care of you and your body. Always honor anything you do to try and be safe. Even if it does not result in safety, the impetus to try is fundamental to survival.

▶ BUT OTHERS WILL JUDGE

Yes, they will. Because many people are consumed with body shame narratives, and feel in constant competition with others for their worth and value, they may well judge you and your body. Try to remember they struggle, too. If you can, wish them well on their journey, and move on. See if compassion for their struggle helps you in your own. You do not need their approval of you to be able to offer your own.

Learning to trust and cherish your body will take a lot of time and effort. The road will be bumpy. Most of us have been brainwashed about our body, and how to move and feed it, for a long, long time.

> When I started doing the work of eating disorder recovery, I started to listen to my body and pay attention to how I was feeling and why. With therapy, I've been able to understand what I was doing. It hasn't been easy. It's taken a lot of work and I still sometimes wander off the path and go to food to calm the storms I'm experiencing. But I know recovery is not linear. It's not ever the upward trend line of a graph. Recovery looks more like the spikes and dips of an EKG. As I recover and grow, the distance between the dips gets larger, and that's what counts.

As you progress and reclaim your felt sense of the world, and as body shame lessens, you may realize how much you have missed. And hopefully, how unwilling you are to go back to the narratives of body shame. You need to grieve these losses and find support in your community. In the next chapter, we will look at how such support, and many other things, make for resiliency in recovery.

▶ BIBLIOGRAPHY

Aamodt, S. (2016, May 6). Why you can't lose weight on a diet. *New York Times*. Retrieved from www.nytimes.com/2016/05/08/opinion/sunday/why-you-cant-lose-weight-on-a-diet.html.

Anderson, L. M., Reilly, E. E., Schaumberg, K., Dmochowski, S., & Anderson, D. A. (2016). Contributions of mindful eating, intuitive eating, and restraint to BMI, disordered eating, and meal consumption in college students. *Eating and Weight Disorders*, *21*(1), 83–90. Retrieved from http://doi.org/10.1007/x40519-015-0210-3.

Bacon, L. (2010). *Health at every size: The surprising truth about your weight*. Dallas, TX: BenBella Books.

Bacon, L. (2014). *Body respect: What conventional health books get wrong, leave out, and just plain fail to understand about weight*. Dallas, TX: BenBella Books.

Bacon, L., & Aphramor, L. (2011). Weight science: Evaluating the evidence for a paradigm shift. *Nutrition Journal*, *10*, 9. Retrieved from http://doi.org/10.1186/1475-2891-10-9.

Beiluz, J., & Haubursin, C. (2018, January 3). The science is in: Exercise won't help you lose much weight. *Vox*. Retrieved from www.vox.com/2018/1/3/16845438/exercise-weight-loss-myth-burn-calories.

Bush, H., Rossy, L., Mintz, L. B., & Schopp, L. (2014). Eat for life: A worksite feasibility study of a novel mindfulness-based intuitive eating intervention. *American Journal of Health Promotion, 29*(6), 380–388. Retrieved from http://doi.org/10.4278/ajhp.120404-QUAN-186.

Campos, P. F. (2012, October 25). Why the "war on fat" is a scam to peddle drugs. *Salon*. Retrieved from www.salon.com/2012/10/25/why_the_war_on_fat_is_a_scam_to_peddle_drugs/.

Chastain, R. (2011a). Do 95% of dieters really fail? *Dances with Fat*. Retrieved from https://danceswithfat.wordpress.com/2011/06/28/do-95-of-dieters-really-fail/.

Chastain, R. (2011b). Calories in/calories out? Science says no. *Dances with Fat*. Retrieved from https://danceswithfat.wordpress.com/2011/06/02/calories-incalories-out-science-says-no/.

Chastain, R. (2011c). Why don't you like my studies? *Dances with Fat*. Retrieved from https://danceswithfat.wordpress.com/2013/12/09/why-dont-you-like-my-studies/.

Chastain, R. (2012). National weight control registry—skydiving without a chute. *Dances with Fat*. Retrieved from https://danceswithfat.wordpress.com/2012/12/27/national-weight-control-registry-skydiving-without-a-chute/.

Chastain, R. (2014). Seriously, weight loss doesn't work. *Dances with Fat*. Retrieved from https://danceswithfat.wordpress.com/2014/06/07/seriously-weight-loss-doesnt-work/.

Chastain, R. (2015). Why do dieters gain their weight back? *Dances with Fat*. Retrieved from https://danceswithfat.wordpress.com/2015/03/05/why-do-dieters-gain-their-weight-back/.

Denny, K. N., Loth, K., Eisenberg, M. E., & Neumark-Sztainer, D. (2013). Intuitive eating in young adults: Who is doing it, and how is it related to disordered eating behaviors? *Appetite, 60*(1), 13–19. Retrieved from http://doi.org/0.1016/j.appet.2012.09.029.

Flegal, K. M., & Graubard, B. I. (2009). Estimates of excess deaths associated with body mass index and other anthropometric variables. *American Journal of Clinical Nutrition, 89*(4), 1213–1219. Retrieved from http://doi.org/10.3945/ajcn.2008.26698.

Flegal, K. M., Kit, B. K., Orpana, H., & Graubard, B. I. (2013). Association of all-cause mortality with overweight and obesity using standard body mass index categories: A systematic review and meta-analysis. *Journal of the American Medical Association*, *309*(1), 71–82. Retrieved from http://doi.org/10.1001/jama.2012.113905.

Harding, K. (2009). All diets work the same: Poorly. *Shapely Prose*. Retrieved from https://kateharding.net/2009/02/26/all-diets-work-the-same-poorly/.

Mann, T., Tomiyama, A. J., Westling, E., Lew, A. M., Samuels, B., & Chatman, J. (2007). Medicare's search for effective obesity treatments: Diets are not the answer. *American Psychology*, *62*(3), 220–233. Retrieved from http://doi.org/10.1037/0003-066X.62.3.220.

Massey, A., & Hill, A. J. (2012). Dieting and food craving: A descriptive, quasi-prospective study. *Appetite*, *58*(3), 781–785. Retrieved from http://doi.org/10.1016/j.appet.2012.01.020.

Matz, J., & Frankel, E. (2006). *The diet survivor's handbook: 60 lessons in eating, acceptance and self-care.* Chicago, IL: Sourcebooks Inc.

Matz, J., & Frankel, E. (2014). *Beyond a shadow of a diet: The comprehensive guide to treating binge eating disorder, compulsive eating, and emotional overeating.* New York, NY: Routledge.

Miller, W. C. (1999). How effective are traditional dietary and exercise interventions for weight loss? *Medicine and Science in Sports & Exercise*, *31*, 1129–1134. Retrieved from www.ncbi.nlm.nih.gov/pubmed/10449014.

O'Hara, L. (2012a). The HAES˙ files: Uncommon knowledge about changes in body weight—part 1. *Health at Every Size˙ Blog*. Retrieved from http://healthateverysizeblog.org/2012/05/page/6.

O'Hara, L. (2012b). The HAES˙ files: Uncommon knowledge about changes in body weight—part 2. *Health at Every Size˙ Blog*. Retrieved from http://healthateverysizeblog.org/2012/05/page/3.

Parker-Pope, T. (2011, December 28). The fat trap. *New York Times Magazine*. Retrieved from www.nytimes.com/2012/01/01/magazine/tara-parker-pope-fat-trap.html.

Pontzer, H. (2017). The exercise paradox. *Scientific American*, *316*(2), 26–31.

Pontzer, H., Durazo-Arvizu, R., Dugas, L. R., Plange-Rhule, J., Bovet, P., Forrester, T. E., Lambert, E. V., Cooper, R. S., Schoeller, D. A., & Luke, A. (2016). Constrained total energy expenditure and metabolic adaptation to physical activity in adult humans. *Current Biology, 26*(3), 410–417. Retrieved from http://dx.doi.org/10.1016/j.cub.2015.12.046.

Pontzer, H., Raichlen, D. A., Wood, B. M., Mabulla, A. Z. P., Racette, S. B., & Marlowe, F. W. (2012). Hunter-gatherer energetics and human obesity. *PLOS One,* Retrieved from http://doi.org/10.1371/journal.pone.0040503.

Puhl, R. M., & Heuer, C. A. (2010). Obesity stigma: Important considerations for public health. *American Journal of Public Health, 100*(6), 1019–1028.

Puhl, R. M., Luedicke, J., & Heuer, C. A. (2013). The stigmatizing effect of visual media portrayals of obese persons on public attitudes: Does race or gender matter? *Journal of Health Communication, 18*(7), 805–826. Retrieved from http://doi.org/10.1080/10810730.2012.757393.

Reiner, M., Niermann, C., Jekauc, D., & Woll, A. (2013). Long-term health benefits of physical activity—A systematic review of longitudinal studies. *BMC Public Health, 13*, 813. Retrieved from http://doi.org/10.1186/1471-2458-13-813.

Ross, R., & Janssen, I. (2001). Physical activity, total and regional obesity: Dose-response considerations. *Medicine and Science in Sports and Exercise, 33*, Supplement 6, S521–S527.

Shouse, S. H., & Nilsson, J. (2011). Self-silencing, emotional awareness, and eating behaviors in college women. *Psychology of Women Quarterly, 35*, 451–457. Retrieved from http://journals.sagepub.com/doi/abs/10.1177/0361684310388785.

Thomas, D. M., Bouchard, C., Church, T., Slentz, C., Kraus, W. E., Redman, L. M., . . . Heymsfield, S. B. (2012). *Obesity Review, 13*(10), 835–847. Retrieved from http://doi.org/10.1111/j.1467-789X.2012.01012.x.

Toler, M. (2016). The Binge Eating Disorder Association Annual Conference. Retrieved from https://www.melissatoler.com/.

Tomiyama, A. J., Ahlstrom, B., & Mann, T. (2013). Long-term effects of dieting: Is weight loss related to health? *Social and Personality Psychology Compass, 7*(12), 861–877. Retrieved from www.dishlab.org/pubs/2013%20Compass.pdf.

Tribole, E., & Resch, E. (2012). *Intuitive eating: A revolutionary program that works.* New York, NY: St. Martin's Griffin.

Wadden, T. A., & Stunkard, A. J. (1986). Controlled trial of very low calorie diet, behavior therapy, and their combination in the treatment of obesity. *Journal of Consulting and Clinical Psychology, 54*(4), 482–488. Retrieved from http://dx.doi.org/10.1037/0022-006X.54.4.482.

Wolf, N. (1990). *The beauty myth.* Toronto, ON: Random House.

6

Staying on the Road of Recovery (Even When You Hit a Pothole)

"What did I just do?" I wondered to myself as the nurse rolled me in a bariatric wheelchair toward the exit of the hospital. Shame rushed through my body and I wanted to hide.

"I'm doing this to improve my health and live a long life for my kids," I kept telling myself while I waited for my ride home. I had decided months ago lap band surgery would be my last opportunity to lose weight and remain alive.

I had experienced congestive heart failure, nearly dying, after the birth of my first son and gestational diabetes during my second pregnancy. I worried about my weakened heart with my family history and polycystic ovary syndrome, which affects hormonal and metabolic systems. The odds favored me developing diabetes at some point, which added to my distress.

To rationalize my decision, I divided the eating disorder and my body weight in my mind. With several years of strong recovery from BED under my belt, I had convinced myself I was emotionally, mentally, and psychologically prepared to pursue weight loss once again. It was a very black and white decision for me at the time: I would have surgery, lose weight, and be around for my kids, or else I would die.

Living with the lap band proved to be an entirely a negative experience. It encouraged the eating disorder behaviors I had worked so hard to move past in prior years and introduced me to new ways to engage in a disordered relationship with food and body. It also reinforced what I knew to be true, but ignored: no matter how much I tried to manipulate my size, when I ate the amount of food needed for my body to function properly, it would revert to its highest weight given its amazing ability to adhere to a set point. I would never be able to nourish myself properly with a silicone band around my stomach or by restricting food to the extent diets required.

Recovery never happens in a straight line and one never knows where the twists and turns will lead. For me, weight loss surgery meant a big step backward, but once I got my bearings, I realized I would need to push forward and figure out how to find recovery again. I continued working with my therapist and began to think about what else I needed.

"What would you think if I started an organization that would help people like me who have eating disorders?" I asked my husband, Ryan, one day in the spring of 2008. The pharmaceutical company I worked for had recently been sold to a larger organization and I was eager, professionally, to do something different.

At the time, I had been reading many academic journal articles about eating disorders and came across a study that showed BED was the most common eating disorder. This shocked me. For some years, I attended conferences and lobby days hosted by organizations that represented the eating disorders community, but never saw people in higher weight bodies or heard discussions about BED. There would sometimes be discussions about "obesity," but never about BED.

There was a gaping hole in the community and I longed for a place where I fit. I asked myself why BED was not being discussed and why, incredibly, it did not have an official diagnosis in the *Diagnostic and Statistical Manual of Mental Disorders* published by the American Psychiatric Association. There are many people with no awareness they have an eating disorder because, like me, they do not fit the stereotype of a white, emaciated, teenage girl. We were in the shadows and there was no mechanism for us to find one another.

Ryan stood behind my decision to start an organization dedicated to those with BED and on June 27, 2008, the Binge Eating Disorder

Association (BEDA) was incorporated. The founding board of BEDA consisted of clinicians I knew and trusted, and a few who were recommended to me by colleagues affiliated with other eating disorder organizations. My co-author, Amy Pershing, is one such person and was recommended to me by Judith Banker, past president of the Academy of Eating Disorders. I am forever grateful to Judith because from Amy and a few other board members, I learned about Health at Every Size (HAES®), a paradigm that would become a major part of the final pieces of my recovery.

The first several times I heard about the HAES® paradigm, I embraced the ideas, but thought it might be too radical for the eating disorders community. I knew many people resisted the idea that higher weight individuals with eating disorders should not pursue weight loss. As the new kid on the block, I did not want to make too many waves too soon.

As time went by and I became more comfortable with the concept of HAES® in my own life, the BEDA board and I began to adopt the principles as a foundational set of beliefs from which we would work. I experienced, with the help of HAES®, a shift in my own thinking that included less self-judgment and shame, and more joy.

I would need to approach recovery in a different way going forward. Learning to trust my body and its internal cues felt scary, especially with the lap band in place. This new approach to recovery would take a long time and be uncomfortable, but for the first time I had hope. I learned empathy for my Self, my body, and the journey.

As I became more confident and less fearful in my recovery and journey, I developed into a more passionate and outspoken advocate for those with BED and in higher weight bodies with any type of eating disorder. In response to conversations I heard among eating disorder clinicians who had no concept of their own thin privilege or awareness of how they stigmatized weight, I began to share my experiences to help them understand how detrimental this way of thinking is for their eating disorder clients.

Two years ago, I had my lap band removed. Walking out the doors of the bariatric center nine years after the original surgery without a silicone band around my stomach was liberating. It took me that long to overcome my own internalized biases around weight to insist on its removal. Despite all my recovery work, I still feared being viewed as a failure by the bariatric surgeon and his staff. I also knew removing the band would require another phase of recovery to authentically connect with my body cues and tolerate the inevitable changes in my body, but I was ready.

Finding my voice and speaking my truth helped heal parts of me I was unaware existed before this journey began. Recovered does not mean we never have another eating disorder thought or even act on them occasionally, but it does mean we have a place from which to weather the storm. I am grateful for the home my body has become and I cherish it daily to the best of my ability.

▶ WHAT IS RECOVERY?

> It is no surprise that danger and suffering surround us. What astonishes is the singing.
>
> —Jack Gilbert

Defining recovery from binge eating disorder is, surprisingly, a difficult thing to do. There is no clinical standard for "recovered." Does it mean never binge eating again? Does it mean always being at peace with one's body, and always eating in an attuned way? Does it ever mean weight loss or shape change? Does it look the same for everyone? Does it ebb and flow, or remain constant?

In my own journey, I have changed how I define "recovered" many times. Over the years in my clinical practice I have found that recovery, and the very process of change itself, looks different for different people. For many, it is a gradual shift from making food and movement choices out of shame and fear to making food and movement choices from a place of compassion, protection, and joy. For some, it means a virtual cessation of binge behaviors. For others, it means an occasional recurrence of binge eating in times of significant stress. Sometimes, it is a gradual limiting of the severity and duration of behaviors, but some binge eating remains. While many programs and books suggest full recovery is possible, I think we must take care not to shame whatever that may look like for each of us. Recovery is about course correction, not perfection. It is about what comes *next* after a bump in the road. In fact, it cannot be perfect; perfectionism is part of what maintains binge eating in the first place, and drives the diet paradigm. Expecting perfection is a denial of the complexity, and much of the joy, of being human.

▶ WHAT'S IN A WORD?

For some people, the word "recovered" comes to feel like the right description for where they are in their journey with BED. For others, "in recovery" better describes the end result. And for still others, there is little value in a "measurement" of their "progress" at all. My colleague Carmen Cool, a psychotherapist, teacher, and HAES® advocate, uses "recovered," and describes it this way:

> I define recovered as choices I make coming from love, not from fear or shame. There is congruence between what I say I believe and how I live. My choices are grounded in my body's wisdom—they are mine, as opposed to either complying with a diet or rebelling against one. Part of being recovered, too, is moving away from a kind of thinking that privileges one body type over another. In terms of behavior, I think what matters is the "then what." For example, several years ago my family was in town and my partner and I had lunch with them. Afterwards, I felt pretty activated by the visit. My partner and I left the restaurant and walked down the street and I thought, I need chicken wings. We had just had lunch. I knew I wasn't hungry. But we went to have wings. It was so obvious that it was emotional and I found it oddly hilarious that I was doing it while being so aware of what it was all about. What was important was what happened next. Not "now I can't eat dinner." Not "might as well keep bingeing." No self-hatred. It was just a moment, and then back to connection with my Self. I don't think recovered means never eating in a disconnected way, or bingeing. It's all about what comes *next*.

▶ EMBRACING WISE VULNERABILITY

> I was sure that once I had my act together, I would be loved. I now know it's not my "act" that people love. Recovery let me allow the love in that was waiting all along.

As we've seen, much of the driving force behind the development of BED is learning from many voices over time that our fundamental feelings, thoughts, and body are not acceptable, or only conditionally so. We learn through shame and fear to disconnect from Self; much of the truth of our stories goes underground in order to maintain the connections we need to survive. We learn to treat food and movement in the same way, behaving as we think we should to attain (or maintain) a specific body size or shape. This, as I have seen in both clinical practice and personal experience, is not about something truly being wrong or broken. It is what we needed to do to survive. As such, we deeply buy into the idea that keeping ourselves hidden from view, be it our feelings, desires, and passions or our bodies themselves, is the best strategy to avoid further damage. Recovery asks us to do the exact opposite. It asks us to be the one thing we have been told not to be: authentically who we are.

Stepping increasingly into Self requires we live in a space of what I call wise vulnerability. Wise vulnerability refers to taking a *well-considered* risk of being authentic in the world, often with little control over how we are received. Such risk requires self-compassion, courage, and considerable care in choosing those we allow closest to us. Wise vulnerability requires that in sharing ourselves with others, we know that if we are judged, it is not about our worth but about the situation. Wise vulnerability requires knowing we will survive loss and the experience of shame and fear.

The most important thing for long-term recovery is to believe we are enough to be loved, *as is*. Not when we've lost weight, not when we've jumped through the right hoops, but right now. When we realize we are worthy, that some parts of our story are learned and not truth, we can risk "imperfection." When we risk imperfection, we can connect authentically. We finally feel seen and heard. We can survive the inevitable loss and hurt of life because we are not alone. We can endure losing relationships sometimes, and can navigate the occasional conflict in good relationships, too. *When we know we can survive pain, we can change our relationship to food.* We can soothe by allowing the one thing we have needed all along: compassionate community.

In the process of recovering from the devastation of BED, I have become aware, however tentatively, that there are people in my life who actually care about me. Beyond just the polite wave and "Hello, there." These individuals want to see my art, hear my songs, listen to my stories. They claim that they are interested in me, the way I think, the things I value. Sometimes, one of them will actually call me on the phone or email to see when we can get together, just to be together! This is quite a shock to me. I didn't believe it for a long time.

▶ DEEPENING RECOVERY

As recovery deepens over time, a number of things change. We are increasingly able to tolerate all the parts of who we are. We are able to build a self-compassionate narrative about the past, and grieve losses. We can allow the grief of time lost trying to "fix" our bodies, and the energy expended in shame. We begin to live in Self more and more, with integrity and purpose, remembering who we wanted to be. We work less on healing and more on being, speaking our needs as we go. We are "real" more often, and can allow intimacy while effectively soothing fear or shame narratives. And we can tolerate being part of a group without fear of loss of self.

> It's so different now. I'm sitting with the urge to binge. I stop, breathe, go in. It's like a wake-up call now. I realize that old desire to get away from my anger. I want to stuff it; of course, I want to. That kept me alive when my father was violent. As I allow that sensation, I notice that I don't really want to stuff it anymore. Now I actually want to scream. I feel my lungs filling up; I'm letting my voice go. The windows rattled, the dog jumped. And I scream and scream. I am still here. I am OK. It is now, not then. I am still here. I have survived another wave. Now I can hear what I really need, and act on it from Self.

As recovery takes hold, we come to know we can handle the negative. We increasingly notice present-day experiences of oppression, and we allow feelings of anger, hurt, and betrayal instead of internalizing the narrative. We experience loss, heartache, or rejection without becoming triggered into abandonment narratives and the need to binge. We can increasingly own mistakes and address shame activation that may result without going to food. We ask for and offer help in balance, and slowly end or limit toxic relationships in our lives. And we keep coming back to hope for change, stepping back into Self, even when the world feels dark and scary.

Further, we develop wisdom about our body over time and make choices from both in-the-moment desire and overall needs. We increasingly recognize hunger, fullness, pain, sensuality, sexuality, and the desire for movement. We gently course correct instead of relapse, and learn what is there to be learned from the experience. We overeat or under-eat at times without activation of a diet/binge cycle, and keep our own wisdom about food and weight in the face of others' behaviors or judgments. We move for joy and well-being (or choose not to move at all). Protecting our body, not weight change, is the goal. Beauty, to the degree we find it of interest, is increasingly on our own terms and a source of joy and play.

We may also come to know that aging, sickness, pain, and even mortality, are part of the journey of life and not rebellion by a misbehaving body. We can come to see that food moralization and the medicalization of weight (and of many normative processes like aging) is about the fear of having very limited control of what happens to us ultimately. People with enough resources can hide from this truth longer by buying in (literally) to the idea of being able to overrule our bodies with enough restriction, or elimination of the latest danger food or the right cleanse. Sadly, health has become another "thin," something we must all be striving to attain. To not be doing so is tantamount to letting oneself "go," to giving up, to being ultimately a lesser person. Again, those who do not participate are blamed and shamed for any disease or evidence of aging.

In recovery, the paradigm must change. When we feel body shame, we increasingly label the feeling for what it is—fear of not being good enough— and move toward the fear with compassion and kindness. There is no right pace, no timetable, for recovery. Each and every step matters.

> Much fuss is made in our culture about not wasting time: making every minute count. Sometimes, I'm relieved that in reality, calendar time doesn't actually have anything to do with quality of life. Recovery from binge eating disorder takes a lot of time. What matters is that I get to emerge from the detritus that keeps me all tangled and covered over. By doing the work, as I am able, not rushing forward, not accelerating the pace of recovery by sheer willpower, I gain more ground, little bit by little bit. It all adds up.

▶ CHALLENGES FROM OUR INNER WORLD

There are many internal challenges in BED recovery, things with which we must come to terms. Building an awareness of your particular triggers helps smooth the way. For example, you will likely hear your inner dieter in times of stress or fear, or go to food sometimes when a younger part is activated and takes over. Once again, this is not a relapse or a failure; it is an old, powerful safety mechanism. Draw on POWR, step back into Self when you are able, and meet your parts with tenderness.

For many people, letting go of the idea they are "damaged" or "dysfunctional" is in and of itself a challenge. Sometimes, having a "problem" like binge eating has been the only proof that we have endured pain. Binge eating has allowed us to hang onto the truth that not everything was (or is) OK. Being recovered, however, doesn't mean *giving in* to family or cultural mythology. Quite to the contrary, recovery means *saying* the truth from Self, relieving our angry teenage part from the burden of carrying our story by acting it out. Recovery does not mean we "get over it" or forget what happened. It means we make space for our feelings as they occur, we listen to them, and care for ourselves increasingly with compassion and gentle good care. Recovery may mean forgiveness of those who are truly remorseful for the pain they have caused. Or it may mean acceptance of the reality of what happened when forgiveness is not an option. We may work on this healing always.

Holly Brewer, a singer/songwriter and political activist, talks about a metaphor for dealing with past trauma that resonates with many of my clients. In a video interview on *The Fifth Estate* (2003), Holly compared past trauma to a book. At some point, we may need to close the cover and move on, but we can do so only after we have read and understood this book to the best of our ability. By closing it and putting it on our shelf, we do not forget it is there, nor do we hope to destroy it. In fact, it will be there always as part of our library. It may be opened and re-examined at any time. But, when we choose to close and shelve the book, we are honoring that this volume does not define our whole library, or stop us from adding other volumes as we go.

Recovery also asks us to inhabit, move, and protect the body we live in right now, even if it hurts, even if it is ill, no matter its shape or size. It asks us to care for and protect this body of ours as best we are able, and notice changes that may happen along the way. Recovery means body shame messages are labeled as learned oppression, not truth. If being bigger has been psychologically equated with safety, recovery asks us to find safety and power in other ways. If being smaller has meant being more attractive, recovery asks us to redefine our ideas about beauty. And recovery asks us to make these changes *whether our body changes in the process of healing or not.*

Finally, recovery ultimately asks us to remember who we wanted to be. How has your voice been put on hold? Where have you sacrificed your dreams, joys, and desires? What are the dangers in thriving instead of surviving? Of living a life increasingly in tune with what you really, truly want? And can you challenge whatever might be in the way? Can you identify what you can control, and what systems of oppression may limit your options? Can you take some role to create change in these systems? And if not, can you let go of self-blame?

Despite what the recovery movement may suggest, in my experience, no one recovers completely. Being recovered, as you may define it for yourself, does not mean there are no scars remaining and no evidence of what you have survived. You grow and heal as best you are able, increasingly allowing desire, joy, and hope to guide your way. We cannot repair everything such that it appears we have never suffered at all. To hope for this as the goal denies our stories, and denies being human. We cannot reclaim some life we might have lived had everything been different. To expect this robs us of the celebration of the bumpy, imperfect healing we are amazingly able to do.

▶ HOLDING TRUTH

> We can stand up and say no at any point, even if we've been saying yes our entire lives.
>
> —Lidia Yuknavitch

In our current cultural milieu, recovery and body acceptance is in many ways a radical act. Coping with the sociocultural injustice of weight stigma is fundamental to healing internalized shame; this is where many treatment paradigms can fail. Often, the onus for healing falls solely on the person with BED and their inner psychological world; this allows weight stigma and other forms of oppression off the proverbial hook. Once again the whole truth about—and reason for—binge eating is fractured and part of it denied.

Binge eating is to some degree an *appropriate* response to the traumas of weight stigma and oppression, given the internalization of shame. If we stop shaming ourselves for the size and shape of our bodies, it means we can challenge the thought distortions and negative internal messages we've learned. From there, we can collectively challenge the multi-billion dollar industry attached to weight loss. If we are serious about ending eating disorders generally, we must end weight stigma and thin privilege. And we do that first by becoming angry instead of ashamed.

It is critical to remember that holding such truth is a tremendous amount of psychological and somatic work, especially at first. Sometimes we can hang in and fight the good fight; sometimes we need to back away and take a break. As any Buddhist can attest, no one stays forever "on the mat." We need to disconnect, to check-out, to waste time, distract, even go to food sometimes, and then, refreshed, we can circle the wagons once more. This is not pathology; it is the nature of change.

▶ THE RESOURCES TO RECOVER

Without doubt, recovery works best in a physically and emotionally safe environment with adequate resources, access to a wide variety of food and movement options, access to treatment, adequate time to focus on the work of healing, and others you trust who are available to support your efforts. For many people, such a situation is far from possible. Due to lack of access to health care, lack of time to focus on recovery, food deserts, lack of understanding about BED and weight bias from referring professionals, and limited availability of BED-specific treatment, many people have trouble starting or sustaining their healing. Sadly, it currently requires coming from a place of privilege to even begin the journey. Powerful forces like poverty, racism, homophobia, gender binarism, misogyny, ableism, cultural appropriation and obliteration impact our ability to heal and find self-compassion. Thus, where we are able to do so, adding our voice to the work of change and advocacy is empowering and healing.

▶ BUILDING COMMUNITY

Whenever we are challenging dominant paradigms, be they our internal critic voice or the external voice of cultural oppression, a powerful tool in the survival toolbox is finding like-minded people. Having a group or network to turn to for venting feelings, talking through new ideas, and strategizing how to balance self-care and advocacy/growth efforts is vitally important. Community allows us to know we are not alone anymore (as we may have been for a long time), unites our efforts into more powerful action, and allows us to feel hope.

I cannot tell you just how important finding a non-diet support group was for me at the beginning of my recovery journey. I learned how to rely on others' strength when I needed to take a break, how to get back up from a stumble, and how to offer my voice when others needed help to keep going. I finally learned firsthand that people can support and care for each other, share difficult feelings, endure conflict, and still have each other's backs.

Social anxiety can make finding community even more difficult. Take steps as you are able. Start perhaps with an online community or group. Or consider taking a workshop on recovery, a class on social justice, or just begin with reading more about others who have gone through experiences of trauma. Appendix A has some resources to help you begin.

▶ USING YOUR VOICE

What can you do to change such an entrenched system? There is no right work, no right amount of time to devote, no one way to add your voice. You may write letters or blogs, post on social media, give talks, teach. Or you may make your impact by wearing what you love no matter your shape or size. Swim at the beach without apology, play with your kids on the swing, or eat a cookie in public. Refuse to be weighed at the doctor's office unless there is medical *necessity*. Refuse/refute diet talk. Move as though you cherished your body right now. Keep compassion for your judgmental part—it comes from honest fear—and own it when you hurt others. Honor others' journeys as different from your own.

> I learned to believe my body wasn't OK. So did my daughters, from me. Now, when I feel my body judgment voice, I know it's just about fear of not being acceptable. My job when that happens is not to change my body, but to help change the world. And to bring my daughters, and my son, with me.
>
> For me, binge eating was about denying my sexual orientation and non-binary gender identity. I was trying to not look like either

gender, just hoping for amorphous, and denying my whole self. I am still fighting every day for the most basic rights. But the fight is not to change myself. Now, it is to challenge the status quo. If I dress "feminine" and someone else is uncomfortable, that is theirs to change. Or not.

Ultimately, it is about taking the risk each moment to see if recovery is worth the work.

Recovery is about the wonder of feeling less anxious, happier, stronger, better, lighter. It takes practice and time to acclimate to this new way of being. Which of course is not a static state. The good, great, amazing news is that I do feel better, lighter (not necessarily physically), stronger, less anxious. Better able to remember to access my adult Self when faced with a conundrum. Quite amazing. And, as I take a breath to sit with it, walk in it, stretch in that space, I am fully amazed and so grateful for the way it feels right now.

Why do the heavy psychological lifting of recovery from BED? What you have to gain is not simply an end to binge eating. In fact, binge eating is a symptom of where we are living out of integrity with our own stories. Recovery is nothing short of reclaiming all that has been stuffed down, at last gently stepping into our lives, tolerating inevitable vulnerability and uncertainty. Tara Brach quotes Zen Master Charlotte Joko Beck to explain how healing allows us to

develop the power and courage to return to that which we have spent a lifetime hiding from, to rest in the bodily experience of the present moment—even if it is a feeling of being humiliated, of failing, of abandonment, of unfairness. Even perhaps, of joy.

May we each, and together, find our way home.

▶ BIBLIOGRAPHY

Brach, T. (2004). *Radical acceptance: Embracing your life with the heart of a Buddha*. New York, NY: Bantam.

The Fifth Estate. (2003). Spiritual shepherds. Canadian Broadcast Corporation. Retrieved from www.cbc.ca/fifth/blog/spiritual-shepherds.

Friedan, B. (2013). *The feminine mystique* (50th Anniversary Ed.). New York, NY: W. W. Norton & Company, Inc.

Gilbert, J. (2012). Horses at midnight without a moon. In *Collected Poems*. New York, NY: Alfred A. Knopf.

Nepo, M. (2000). *The book of awakening: Having the life you want by being present to the life you have*. Newburyport, MA: Conari Press.

Nepo, M. (2006). *The exquisite risk: Daring to live an authentic life*. New York, NY: Three Rivers Press.

Walker, A. (2004). *In search of our mothers' gardens*. New York, NY: Mariner Books.

Whyte, D. (2003). *Everything is waiting for you*. Langley, WA: Many Rivers Press.

Wolf, N. (1991). *The beauty myth*. Toronto, ON: Random House.

Yuknavitch, Lidia (2017, October 24). *The misfit's manifesto*. Simon & Schuster/ TED Books.

Appendix A

Online Resources for Community Building

1. Beauty Redefined: http://beautyredefined.com

2. Association for Size Diversity and Health: http://sizediversityand health.org

3. National Eating Disorders Association: http://nationaleatingdis orders.org

4. The Body Positive: http://thebodypositive.org

5. Dances With Fat: http://danceswithfat.wordpress.com

6. Melissa Fabello: http://melissafabello.com

7. Food Psych Podcast: http://christyharrison.com/foodpsych

8. The Body Is Not an Apology: http://thebodyisnotanapology.com

9. Amy Pence Brown: www.amypencebrown.com

10. Health at Every Size: http://haescommunity.com

11. Council on Size and Weight Discrimination: http://cswd.org

12. About Face: http://about-face.org

13. Dr. Deah's Body Shop: http://drdeah.com

14. Fattitude: http://fattitudethemovie.com

15. Overcoming Overeating Online Support: http://overcomingover eating.com

16. Nalgona Positivity Pride: http://nalgonapositivitypride.com

17. Be Nourished: http://benourished.org

18. Sister Summer: http://desireeadaway.com/sistersummer

19. Woman Within: http://womanwithin.org

20. National Association for Males with Eating Disorders: http://name dinc.org

Index